A BIBLE STUDY FOR

10 WORDS
TO HEAL OUR
BROKEN WORLD

A BIBLE STUDY FOR

10 WORDS

TO HEAL OUR
BROKEN WORLD

MARRIAGE

JUSTICE

SEX

FREEDOM

HUMAN

AUTHORITY

LOVE

TRUTH

FAITH

BEAUTY

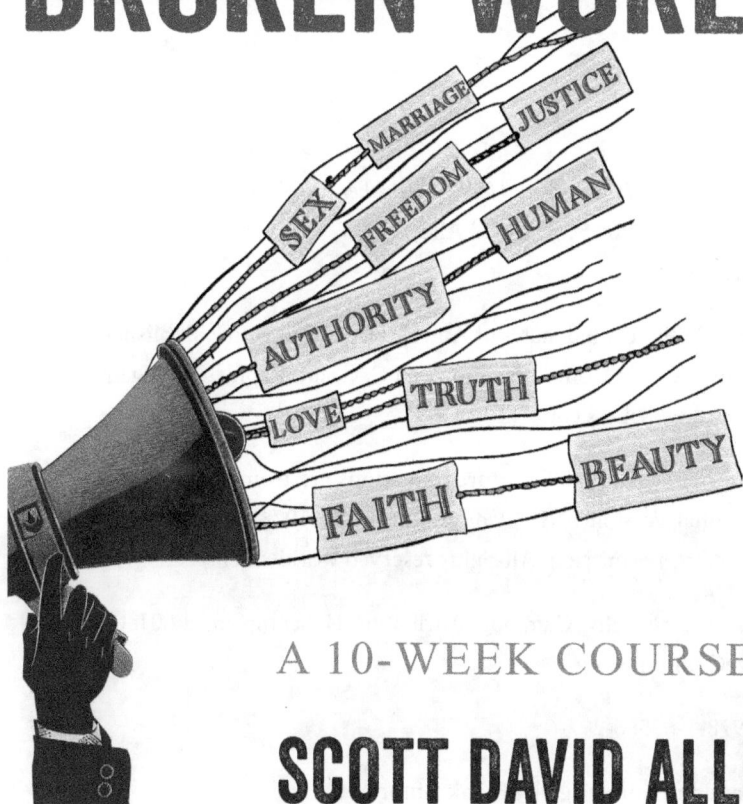

A 10-WEEK COURSE

SCOTT DAVID ALLEN

credo
house publishers

Cover and interior design by Frank Gutbrod
Editing by Donna Huisjen

Printed in the United States of America
First edition

CONTENTS

Welcome *1*

How The Course Works *3*

Sample Group Session *4*

The *10 Words to Heal Our Broken World* Book *5*

1. **Truth** *6*

2. **Human** *24*

3. **Sex** *40*

4. **Marriage** *54*

5. **Freedom** *74*

6. **Authority** *96*

7. **Justice** *118*

8. **Faith** *146*

9. **Beauty** *168*

10. **Love** *188*

About the Author *215*

Endnotes *216*

Additional Resources *221*

WELCOME

This study aims to help you grow your faith by deepening your understanding of ten vital words. Why these words? They are so foundational—so essential. How they are defined and understood will do more to shape a life, a family, or an entire nation, for good or ill, than almost anything else.

We often take words for granted, but we shouldn't. They are incredibly powerful. "In the beginning was the Word, and the Word was with God, and the Word was God," begins the Gospel of John. The Word spoke the universe into being. It's no overstatement to say that we live in a word-based universe.

God created us in his image with the capacity to use words and language to create culture. "Culture lives by language," wrote historian Robert Lewis Wilken, "and the sentiments, thoughts, and feelings of a Christian culture are formed and carried by the language of the Scriptures." If we long to see a revival in our churches and a reformation in our culture, we must recover the biblical definitions of these ten words that have, tragically, been redefined in popular culture.

As my friend and mentor Darrow Miller has taught me, if you want to change culture you must begin by changing language. The enemies of the gospel understand this very well. They have been strategically redefining the ten words that are the focus of this course to change society to reflect their false, destructive ideologies.

Someone will shape the culture by defining words and embedding them into the institutions at the foundations of a culture. If not Christians with true, biblical definitions that lead to freedom and human flourishing, then non-Christians with false redefinitions that destroy nations.

Our calling as followers of Jesus Christ is to bless our broken nations. A significant way we do this is by knowing and defending true definitions. These ten words are not empty vessels to be filled with whatever meaning people wish. These are God-spoken words, and to redefine them is an act of rebellion against the Creator.

Because we are all shaped by the surrounding culture more profoundly than most of us realize, we've likely absorbed false understandings of these ten words to some degree. This is a significant problem because our formation in Christlikeness must be grounded on the proper, biblical meanings of words. That's why I wrote this study—to help open your eyes to the power, beauty, and veracity of biblical words and motivate you to build your life faithfully, based on true definitions. I hope to help equip you to steward, preserve, and pass along these words and meanings to future generations.

So, welcome! I'm so glad you are here.

Scott David Allen

HOW THE COURSE WORKS

HOW THE COURSE WORKS

- This course is designed for personal study, reflection, and learning in community, whether with a few friends around a table, in your small group, in a larger class format, or with your entire church.
- The course is ten sessions long. We recommend one session per week.
- We recommend scheduling a one- to two-hour group meeting for each session, depending on how long you allow for discussion. Group meetings involve watching a 10- to 15-minute video, prayer, and discussion. See the sample session on the following page.
- Each session includes a homework assignment that should be completed before the group meeting. This should take no more than an hour and involves reading and prayerfully reflecting on key Bible passages.
- Each session concludes with a personal reflection and application exercise.
- You will need a copy of this Study Guide to participate. You may order print versions or download free digital PDF versions at *10WordsBook.org.*

Here's what a typical group meeting session could look like.

- Welcome and open with prayer.
- Discuss what you learned during your personal study about the true definition of each word (15 to 20 minutes).
- Course video (10 to 15 minutes)
- Read the true and the false definitions. Discuss the meaning and consequences of the *false* definition (15 to 20 minutes).
- Review the personal application questions together, but answer them on your own.
- Close with prayer.

The 10 Words course is designed to work for various group sizes and in various environments. Your gatherings may include additional elements like a meal or worship time or follow a structure different from this sample. Please adapt as you see fit.

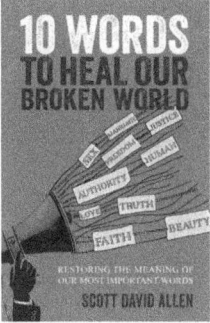

We highly recommend reading the book *10 Words to Heal Our Broken World: Recovering the True Meaning of Our Most Important Words* by Scott David Allen alongside this course, as it will greatly enhance your learning experience. The book contains a chapter for each of the ten words that can be read during the week you are studying the word in this course.

TRUTH

"What is truth?"

This question, famously posed by Pontius Pilate to Jesus during his inquisition, continues to ring down through the ages, right into the present.[1]

Many people today speak of "your truth" or "my truth."

They talk of truth as if it's a personal, private belief.

Is truth what you or I believe, or does it actually exist and have a real, objective meaning?

Charles Chaput states, "Truth exists, whether we like it or not. We don't create the truth; we find it, and we have no power to change it to our tastes."[2]

How do you understand truth?

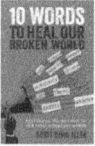

This week we're reading Chapter 1, "Truth," in *10 Words to Heal Our Broken World* by Scott David Allen.

PERSONAL BIBLE STUDY: *TRUTH*

Before You Begin

In the space below write a concise, dictionary-style definition of "truth" from your current understanding without consulting sources such as a dictionary, the internet, or another person. The purpose is to record your current understanding and see how it changes due to this study.

BIBLE STUDY

Read the following passages and prayerfully respond to the question below.

> Your word, LORD, is eternal; it stands firm in the heavens. (Psalm 119:89)

> Every word of God proves true; he is a shield to those who take refuge in him. (Proverbs 30:5 ESV)

> God is not human, that he should lie, not a human being, that he should change his mind. Does he speak and then not act? Does he promise and not fulfill? (Numbers 23:19)

> It is impossible for God to lie. (Hebrews 6:18)

QUESTION: What do these passages teach about the relationship between God and truth?

QUESTION: In your own words, why is God necessary for the concept of truth to exist?

Reflect on these quotes from the *10 Words* book:

Truth requires fixed points of reference that exist apart from our ideas, thoughts, and beliefs. The most obvious fixed point is the world around us. The computer I'm typing on, the desk I'm working at, the chair I'm sitting in. The sky, trees, stars, and galaxies. The cells, atoms, and electrons. These things exist whether or not I believe in them. We study the physical world through science, and, as such, science is a quest for truth, a discovery of what actually exists or is real.

But is there a reality that exists beyond the physical world? A reality as basic, but more ultimate? The physical world itself points to the answer. Every effect must have a sufficient cause. The design and purposefulness of the natural world point to a transcendent, intelligent, purposeful designer. The existence of complex information, such as we find in the DNA molecule, necessitates an author—a great Word behind all words. This is the point that the apostle Paul makes in his letter to the Romans: "Since the creation of the world God's invisible qualities—his eternal power and divine nature—have been clearly seen, being understood from what has been made" (Romans 1:20). The physical world isn't a cosmic accident; it is a creation, and it points to a Creator in a way that is "clearly seen," or, as America's founding fathers put it, "self-evident."

God has revealed himself to us through his creation but also through his words. He spoke to Abraham, Isaac, and Jacob. He spoke to Moses and revealed himself through the prophets. He revealed moral truth on Mount Sinai in the form of the Ten Commandments, which he wrote by his own hand. These truths stand as a fixed moral point for all peoples at all times.

As the church fathers put it, God reveals truth to us in "two books"— the book of God's Word (the Bible), and the book of God's world (creation). We can add to this a third "book," the book of human reason and the internal witness of conscience, or "the law written on the heart" (Romans 2:15). We search out the truth through the careful study of God's creation using the tools and methods of science, as well as through the careful study of God's written Word through the principles of sound hermeneutics and with the indispensable illumination of the Holy Spirit—the "Spirit of truth" (John 16:13).

In the Hebrew Scriptures, the word for truth is translated as emeth, *a noun or adverb meaning firmness, stability, or reliability. God is the firm, fixed, solid foundation for truth. He is the Great Truth behind all truth. Apart from him truth has no meaning. It vanishes in a morass of subjectivism and relativism.*

The adversary, Satan, is referred to in the Bible as "the father of lies." Reflect on these passages and prayerfully respond to the questions below:

"[Satan] was a murderer from the beginning, not holding to the truth, for there is no truth in him. When he lies, he speaks his native language, for he is a liar and the father of lies." (John 8:44)

"The thief comes only to steal and kill and destroy." (John 10:10)

QUESTION: What is the relationship between Satan and truth?

QUESTION: What do Satan's lies result in?

Reflect on these quotes from the *10 Words* book:

Through the Bible we also learn why evil exists. Reality is both physical and spiritual. The spiritual realm is the domain of God, but also of angels. The most powerful of these angelic beings, Satan, rebelled against God before the creation of the world. To modern ears talk of angels and demons sounds crazy. Many people see reality as entirely physical. The spiritual realm is derided as a fantasy, but it is as real as the chair on which you sit. This unseen realm exists all around us.

Satan advances his rebellion against God mainly through deception. Adam and Eve believed his lies in the Garden of Eden, and in so doing, they followed Satan's anti-God rebellion. Fallen humanity has been rebelling ever since. This explains our propensity to lie, deceive, or shade the truth. We commit these offenses, at least in part, out of fear that we might be known as we truly are—as sinners. Like Adam and Eve, we hide from God and from others by lying—by making ourselves out to be something we are not.

God, the source of all life—of all that is good and beautiful—cannot lie. Satan, by contrast, continually lies. His deceptions are behind all of the world's evil, brokenness, chaos, and heartbreak. "[Satan] comes only to steal and kill and destroy," says Jesus in John 10:10. "He was a murderer from the beginning, not holding to the truth, for there is no truth in him. When he lies, he speaks out of his own character, for he is a liar and the father of lies" (John 8:44).

Read the following passages and prayerfully respond to the questions below.

[Jesus said,] "I am the way and the truth and the life." (John 14:6)

To the Jews who had believed him, Jesus said, "If you hold to my teaching, you are really my disciples. Then you will know the truth, and the truth will set you free." (John 8:30–32)

Jesus answered, "You say that I am a king. In fact, the reason I was born and came into the world is to testify to the truth. Everyone on the side of truth listens to me." (John 18:37)

[Jesus said,] "I will ask the Father, and he will give you another advocate to help you and be with you forever—the Spirit of truth . . . When he, the Spirit of truth, comes, he will guide you into all truth." (John 14:16, 17; 16:13)

[Jesus prayed to God the Father on behalf of His followers, saying,] "Sanctify them by the truth; your word is truth." (John 17:17)

QUESTION: What do these passages teach about the relationship between Jesus and truth?

QUESTION: What does the truth result in, according to Jesus?

QUESTION: According to John 18:37, for what purpose did Jesus say he was born and came into the world?

QUESTION: How does Jesus help us to know the truth?

Reflect on these quotes from the *10 Words* book:

In Jesus, ultimate reality became flesh and dwelt among us. Ultimate truth isn't a philosophical abstraction or metaphysical necessity. It is a person—Jesus Christ.

The New Testament word for truth is aletheia, *meaning "to be revealed." The Greek word from which this noun is derived is* lanthano, *which means "to lie hidden." The Greeks (not unlike today's postmodernists) thought that truth was hidden. But according to the Bible, truth is now revealed in Christ. To express this the writers of Scripture added the negative participle a to* lanthano *to get the word* aletheia. *The truth that was hidden is now revealed.*

Jesus was a man like no other. He made claims no other man has made—not Buddha, Muhammad, or Confucius. He claimed not merely to speak the truth but to be the truth.

Read the following passages and prayerfully respond to the questions below.

You shall not give false testimony against your neighbor. (Exodus 20:16).

The Lord detests lying lips, but he delights in people who are trustworthy. (Proverbs 12:22)

Stand firm then, with the belt of truth buckled around your waist. (Ephesians 6:14)

Love does not delight in evil but rejoices with the truth. (1 Corinthians 13:6)

QUESTION: What do these passages teach us about how we should relate to truth?

QUESTION: What is the relationship between being truthful and being trustworthy?

QUESTION: In what ways do you need to "stand firm" in the truth?

Reflect on these quotes from the *10 Words* book:

A commitment to truth-telling is necessary for healthy relationships and a society's basic functioning. Try to imagine a society—a marriage, family, business, organization, or nation—in which everyone lied, all the time. Nobody could be trusted. Things would fall apart quickly. We forget just how important honesty is. A culture that worships a God who is good, who is utterly trustworthy, who cannot lie, will be a culture that highly values honesty in everyday relationships. It will enjoy high levels of trust in its institutions.

Without a commitment to truth, there would be no university. Nor would there be modern science, nor journalism, nor the study of history. There would be no liberal democracy, for without truth government becomes an exercise in raw power. It is no exaggeration to say that without a commitment to truth as revealed, objective, and knowable, there would be no such thing as civilization.[3]

Without truth, everything devolves into chaos or tyranny. Professor Sinan Aral at the Massachusetts Institute of Technology got it exactly right: "Some notion of truth is central to the proper functioning of nearly every realm of human endeavor. If we allow the world to be consumed by falsity, we are inviting catastrophe."

LEARNING TOGETHER: *TRUTH*

Welcome and Opening

- Go around the room and briefly introduce yourself.
- What drew you to this course?
- What are you looking forward to?

Opening Prayer

Opening Discussion

Discuss together what you learned about truth during your personal study. What ideas stood out to you? How did God speak to you through the Scripture?

Watch the Video and Discuss the Questions Below:
Note: You'll find the "truth" video at 10WordsBook.org.

- What insights did you gain from the video about truth?
- What insights did you gain about the redefinition of truth?

Definitions and Discussion

Read the two definitions and quotes below. Discuss the contemporary redefinition of truth and its cultural consequences.

TRUTH
That which accords with factual, objective reality.

TRUTH REDEFINED
(1) An internal, personal, and subjective sense of reality that exists only in the mind. (2) A social construct created to advantage the dominant group.[1]

"There are no facts, only interpretations."—Fredrick Nietzsche[4]

"There is one thing a professor can be absolutely certain of. Almost every student entering the university believes, or says he believes, that truth is relative."—Allan Bloom[5]

Postmodernism, which rejects any notion of universal, objective truth, was preceded by "modernism," or the worldview of secular materialism. Modernism rejected God, the Bible, and spiritual reality as sources of objective truth, yet it retained the material universe as a fixed point of reference for truth. Postmodernism does away with that, also. It asserts that no fixed points exist. Everything is relative, either to the individual or to the "identity group." There are no publicly authoritative facts or truths that transcend groups or cultures. There are only perspectives or interpretations—your truth, or my truth, but no longer the truth.

If there are no fixed points, no boundaries that divide truth from untruth or good from evil, if everything is a matter of perspective or interpretation, then the very concept of objective truth is defined out of existence. Is it any surprise that "post-truth" was selected in 2016 by Oxford Dictionaries as the international word of the year—after a two thousand percent increase in usage from 2015? The dictionary defined "post-truth" as "relating to or denoting circumstances in which objective facts are less influential in shaping public opinion than appeals to emotion and personal belief."[6]

At a societal level, without public truth; without shared understandings of what is real, true, good, or evil; if even words and texts no longer have a shared public meaning, then there is no center around which different groups can communicate, much less unify. We have no way to achieve consensus or to pursue the common good. Rather, we retreat into our "identity group" bubbles and find it almost impossible to speak to each other, much less agree. Post-truth culture thus is marked by disunity, distrust, or even hatred.

"If there is no objective or universal truth, then any claim to have objective truth will be treated as nothing but an attempt by one [group] to impose its own limited, subjective perspective on everyone else. An act of oppression. A power grab."—Nancy Pearcey[7]

In the absence of a shared, objective truth, we are left with competing identity groups jockeying for power through "narrative creation" and perpetuation. Postmodern evangelists sell narratives as truth, but they are highly distorted accounts of current or past events created to achieve particular outcomes. They are conveyed in a manner designed to bypass reason and appeal to emotion—to sway the masses. To ensure that their narratives go unchallenged, powerful elites use an array of methods to silence dissenting voices, including overt censorship, along with charges of "fake news" and "conspiracy theory," as well as attacks against so-called "misinformation," "disinformation," and "malinformation." All of this is the direct result of postmodernism's denial of objective truth.

"You believe that reality is something objective, external, existing in its own right. You also believe that the nature of reality is self-evident. When you delude yourself into thinking that you see something, you assume that everyone else sees the same thing as you. But I tell you, Winston, that reality is not external. Reality exists in the human mind and nowhere else. Not in the individual mind, which can make mistakes and, in any case, soon perishes: only in the mind of the Party, which is collective and immortal. Whatever the Party holds to be the truth is truth. It is impossible to see reality except by looking through the eyes of the Party. That is the fact that you have got to relearn, Winston." —George Orwell from his novel *1984* [8]

Discussion Questions
- How does the redefinition of truth differ from the original, accurate definition? Discuss all that has changed.
- In what ways have you seen or experienced the redefinition of truth?
- What are some of the social and cultural changes that the redefinition of *truth* has brought about? What kinds of changes have resulted in policies and laws?

Personal Reflection and Application
Next week at home, take time to reflect on these areas of application. Read the questions and write down your responses.

Examine your assumptions about truth
Today, the dominant worldview shaping Western culture is postmodernism, a worldview that rejects the concept of objective truth. We now live in a "post-truth" world, and if we are honest we'll discover that it shapes our thinking—even as Christians— more deeply than we may realize. For example, many Christians claim that their faith is personal and subjective. It is "true for me"

but not an objective truth that is true for everyone and the whole of society.

QUESTION: Examine your assumptions about truth. If your thinking about truth is more personal and subjective, I encourage you to repent.[9] God exists—not just as a Christian belief but as a reality for everyone. His Word in Scripture is true, not just for Christians but for everyone, Christian and non-Christian alike.

A consequence of living in a post-truth world is the proliferation of lies, deceptions, spin, and distorted narratives. Today these dominate network news, the internet, and social media. Propaganda has become so pervasive that knowing the truth about almost any matter has become incredibly challenging. Many are tempted to cynically throw up their hands in despair and ask, "Why even bother?"

But as followers of Jesus, we must not fall into this trap. Despair is a sin. Truth exists, and God has called us to be truth-seekers and critical thinkers, not herd-followers.

Truth-seekers welcome questions, encourage dialogue, and keep an open mind. Our grasp of truth will always be partial and limited, since we are finite beings. Uncovering the truth of a matter can be difficult, particularly in our time. Sometimes it takes years of searching, investigating, listening, discussing, and debating. But that is our job. God has filled us with the Spirit of truth and given us the capacity to know it. We honor him by seeking it. This is how we love God "with all [our] mind" (Luke 10:27). We dishonor him by cynically throwing up our hands and asking, "What's the point?"

QUESTION: Have you fallen into the trap of cynicism and despair about knowing the truth regarding things or events? This may be an area you need to repent over.

To strengthen our grasp of the truth, we Christians must strengthen our confidence in the authority of God's Word, the Bible. We must reject the postmodern idea that the Bible, or any other text, has no objective meaning but only a multitude of interpretations. We must grow in our confidence that the truth of the Bible can be known through careful study, the guidance of the Holy Spirit, and the help of respected teachers in the church, past and present.

QUESTION: In what areas do you still harbor doubts about the truthfulness and reliability of the Bible as God's Word? Turn those doubts into specific questions and seek out honest answers. Pray for God's help and seek wise counsel as you seek the truth.

Personal integrity

Our work as ambassadors of truth must begin at the most basic level—with our personal honesty. While none of us is perfect, we must grow in this area. We can have tremendous influence if we are known as trustworthy, honest, and reliable. After all, this is what God is like. He never lies. He is solid and firm, and we are to imitate him. Let's remember the simple but profound truth that honesty leads to trust, which is the glue that binds together relationships— and society. As the world fractures and fragments, we can do our part to push back by strengthening relationships—with our spouses, friends, co-workers, neighbors, and customers—by living honestly.

QUESTION: Are you careful to speak truthfully, to not lie or shade the truth? Do you keep your word, even when it is costly? Do you keep your agreements, contracts, and vows?

Commitment to free speech and civil, open debate

As followers of Jesus, we must affirm the goodness of reason and logic and free, open, and civil discussion and debate. Our post-truth culture has undermined all of these things, while elevating emotion and power tactics, including shaming, silencing, censoring, and threatening. Of course, emotions are a God-given good, but reason must pull the train. Of all people, Christians should be the most outspoken champions of free speech, free and open inquiry, and civil discussion. As Catholic economist Michael Novak put it, "Only when truth is cherished as an imperative does civilization become possible. Only then can human beings enter into rational conversation with one another. For civilization is constituted by conversation. Barbarians bully; civilized people persuade."[10]

QUESTION: What can you do to support free speech and civil, open dialogue in the pursuit of truth? What steps might you take to resist the growing trends of censorship and shaming in our culture?

Speaking out courageously against deadly cultural lies

In our post-truth culture, truth and love have been scandalously separated. For instance, we are told in countless ways that if we fail to accept and affirm people's chosen identities, we fail to love them. If we insist on objective truth, we are branded intolerant "haters." But dividing truth from love will give us neither.

To be silent or passive in the face of destructive, and even deadly, cultural lies is to fail in our Christian duty to love our neighbors. This dereliction of our Christian duty borders on apostasy. According to Charles Chaput, Christians "don't need to publicly renounce their [faith] to be apostates. They simply need to be silent when their [faith] demands that they speak out; to be cowards when Jesus asks them to have courage; to 'stand away' from the truth when they need to work for it and fight for it."[11]

This is a warning that all who claim Christ must heed. Our standard is always to speak the truth in humility and gentleness—but speak it we must.

QUESTION: Where have you felt cultural or peer pressure to remain silent about important cultural or moral issues that are destroying lives and fracturing society? About what issue is God calling you to speak out truthfully, lovingly, and courageously?

Concluding Thoughts

"The Evangelical is not afraid of facts, for he knows that all facts are God's facts; nor is he afraid of thinking, for he knows that all truth is God's truth, and right reason cannot endanger sound faith. He is called to love God with all his mind . . . A confident intellectualism expressive of robust faith in God, whose Word is truth, is part of the historic evangelical tradition. If present-day evangelicals fall short of this, they are false to their own principles and heritage." —J. I Packer[12]

Are you prepared to live within the truth? If so, your light will shine brightly in an ever-darkening world; yours will be the salt that slows its decay. As Christ-followers, we fix our eyes on our Savior, confident that the "truth will win out" because Jesus is on the throne. The devil's lies may confuse us for a time, but the truth of God will prevail.

RECOMMENDED RESOURCES

- *Total Truth: Liberating Christianity from Its Cultural Captivity* by Nancy Pearcey (2008)
- *Finding Truth: 5 Principles for Unmasking Atheism, Secularism, and Other God Substitutes* by Nancy Pearcey (2015)
- *Saving Truth: Finding Meaning and Clarity in a Post-Truth World* by Abdu Murray (2018)
- *Time for Truth: Living Free in a World of Lies, Hype and Spin* by Os Guinness (2000)
- *Truth Decay: Defending Christianity Against the Challenges of Postmodernism* by Douglas Groothuis (2000)
- *True Truth: Defending Absolute Truth in a Relativistic World* by Art Lindsley (2004)

HUMAN

Who am I?

What does it mean to be human?

Am I created by a loving God, in his image, with inherent dignity, worth, and God-given rights, or am I a highly evolved animal—a product of a purposeless process of evolution?

Am I defined primarily by my skin color, sex, or gender identity?

Am I a sovereign, autonomous being, free to determine my true, authentic self without regard to God, the Bible, or even my bodily anatomy?

Am I a complex biological machine?

Who am I?

This is one of the most important questions anyone can ask. Your answer will do more to shape your life—and your society—for better or worse than any other.

 This week we're reading Chapter 2, "Human," in *10 Words to Heal Our Broken World* by Scott David Allen.

PERSONAL BIBLE STUDY: *HUMAN*

Before You Begin

In the space below write a concise, dictionary-style definition of the word *human* from your current understanding without consulting sources such as a dictionary, the internet, or another person. The purpose is to record your current understanding and see how it changes due to this study.

BIBLE STUDY

Read the following passages and prayerfully respond to the question below.

The LORD God formed a man from the dust of the ground and breathed into his nostrils the breath of life, and the man became a living being. (Genesis 2:7)

God created mankind . . . male and female he created them. (Genesis 1:27)

You [God] created my inmost being; you knit me together in my mother's womb. I praise you because I am fearfully and wonderfully made . . . My frame was not hidden from you when I was made in the secret place, when I was woven together in the depths of the earth. Your eyes saw my unformed body; all the days ordained for me were written in your book before one of them came to be. (Psalm 139:13–16)

[God] himself gives everyone life and breath and everything else. (Acts 17:25)

QUESTION: What do these passages reveal about what it means to be human?

Reflect on this quote from the *10 Words* book:

"This life in us . . . however low it flickers or fiercely burns, is still a divine flame which no man dare presume to put out, be his motives ever so humane and enlightened."—Malcolm Muggeridge[1]

Read the following passages and prayerfully respond to the question below.

> God said, "Let us make mankind in our image, in our likeness"
> . . . So God created mankind in his own image, in the image of
> God he created them. (Genesis 1:26–27)

> [Jesus said,] "Are not two sparrows sold for a penny? Yet not
> one of them will fall to the ground outside your Father's care.
> And even the very hairs of your head are all numbered. So
> don't be afraid; you are worth more than many sparrows."
> (Matthew 10:29–31)

QUESTION: What do these passages reveal about what it means to
be human?

Reflect on these quotes from the *10 Words* book:

*God is spirit (John 4:24), so bearing his image does not refer to physical
resemblance. Rather, we resemble God's nonphysical qualities. God is
a person, and so are we. He can think, feel, and reflect, and we can as
well. He is a moral being, and so are we. He uses speech and language,
as we do. He is a creative, working God, and we too are made to
work and create. He is volitional, and so are we. God reigns as King of
heaven and earth, and we too have a realm and a dominion.*

*All people are equal because God creates them in his image. They all
share equally in his nature and attributes. Yet there is also tremendous
diversity. There are two genders, male and female. There are differences
among cultures and languages, differences in temperament, personality,
and gifts. God even gave each of us a unique physical appearance. This*

diversity is a part of God's marvelous plan and intention and should be appreciated and celebrated. Appreciating human diversity sets us free to be the special people God created us to be. These twin biblical truths of human equality and human uniqueness and diversity provide a foundation for thriving human communities.

"We hold these truths to be self-evident, that all men are created equal, that they are endowed by their Creator with certain unalienable rights, that among these are Life, Liberty, and the pursuit of Happiness."—The Declaration of Independence.

Read the following passages and prayerfully respond to the question below.

"I am the LORD your God . . . You shall have no other gods before me." (Exodus 20:2–3)

"Teacher, which is the greatest commandment in the Law?" Jesus replied: "'Love the Lord your God with all your heart and with all your soul and with all your mind.' This is the first and greatest commandment. And the second is like it: 'Love your neighbor as yourself.'" (Matthew 22:36–39)

QUESTION: What do these passages further reveal about what it means to be human?

Reflect on these quotes:
"Question One: What is the chief end of man? Answer: Man's chief end is to glorify God, and to enjoy him forever."—The Westminster Shorter Catechism

"You have made us for yourself, O Lord, and our heart is restless until it finds its rest in you."—Augustine of Hippo[2]

Read the following passages and prayerfully respond to the question below.

God said, "Let us make mankind . . . so that they may rule over the fish in the sea and the birds in the sky, over the livestock and all the wild animals, and over all the creatures that move along the ground." (Genesis 1:26)

God blessed them and said to them, "Be fruitful and increase in number; fill the earth and subdue it. Rule over the fish in the sea and the birds in the sky and over every living creature that moves on the ground." (Genesis 1:28)

The LORD God had formed out of the ground all the wild animals and all the birds in the sky. He brought them to the man to see what he would name them; and whatever the man called each living creature, that was its name. (Genesis 2:19).

The LORD God took the man and put him in the Garden of Eden to work it and take care of it. (Genesis 2:15)

When I consider your heavens, the work of your fingers, the moon and the stars, which you have set in place, what is mankind that you are mindful of them, human beings that you care for them? You have made them a little lower than the angels and crowned them with glory and honor. You made them rulers over the works of your hands; you put everything under their feet: all flocks and herds, and the animals of the wild, the birds in the sky, and the fish in the sea, all that swim the paths of the seas. (Psalm 8:3–8)

For we are God's handiwork, created . . . to do good works, which God prepared in advance for us to do. (Ephesians 2:10)

QUESTION: What do these passages further reveal about what it means to be human?

Reflect on these quotes from the *10 Words* book:

"When God calls creation into being, He announces that it's "very good," but He doesn't announce that it's finished! Creation doesn't come into existence ready-made with schools, art museums, and farms; those are all begging to be unpacked . . . the riches and potential of God's good creation are entrusted to His image bearers. That is our calling and commission."—James K. A. Smith[3]

Human beings have the unique, God-given capacity to leave this world better than they found it—more prosperous, more beautiful.

Read the following passages and prayerfully respond to the question below.

To Adam [God] said, "Because you listened to your wife and ate fruit from the tree about which I commanded you, 'You must not eat from it,' "Cursed is the ground because of you; through painful toil you will eat food from it all the days of your life. It will produce thorns and thistles for you, and you will eat the plants of the field. By the sweat of your brow you will eat your food until you return to the ground, since from it you were taken; for dust you are and to dust you will return." (Genesis 3:17–19)

The LORD saw how great the wickedness of the human race had become on the earth, and that every inclination of the thoughts of the human heart was only evil all the time. (Genesis 6:5)

The [human] heart is deceitful above all things, and beyond cure. Who can understand it? (Jeremiah 17:9)

Just as sin entered the world through one man [Adam], and death through sin, and in this way death came to all people, because all sinned . . . (Romans 5:12)

The wrath of God is being revealed from heaven against all the godlessness and wickedness of people. (Romans 1:18)

As for you, you were dead in your transgressions and sins. (Ephesians 2:1)

QUESTION: What do these passages further reveal about what it means to be human?

Reflect on these quotes from the *10 Words* book:
"The line separating good and evil passes not through states, nor between classes, nor between political parties either—but right through every human heart—and through all human hearts."— Aleksandr Solzhenitsyn from *The Gulag Archipelago*[4]

"We human beings have both a unique dignity as creatures made in God's image and a unique depravity as sinners under his judgment. The former gives us hope; the latter places a limit on our expectations . . . We can behave like God in whose image we were made, only to

descend to the level of beasts. We are able to think, choose, create, love and worship, but also to refuse to think, to choose evil, to destroy, to hate, and to worship ourselves."—John Stott[5]

Read the following passages and prayerfully respond to the question below.

> God so loved the world that he gave his one and only Son, that whoever believes in him shall not perish but have eternal life. (John 3:16)

> God demonstrates his own love for us in this: While we were still sinners, Christ died for us. (Romans 5:8)

> Like the rest, we were by nature deserving of [God's] wrath. But because of his great love for us, God, who is rich in mercy, made us alive with Christ even when we were dead in transgressions— it is by grace you have been saved. (Ephesians 2:3–5)

QUESTION: What do these passages reveal about what it means to be human?

LEARNING TOGETHER: *HUMAN*
Welcome and Opening Prayer

Opening Discussion
Discuss together what you learned during your personal study about what it means to be human. What ideas stood out to you? How did God speak to you through the Scripture?

Watch the Video and Discuss the Questions Below

Note: You'll find the "human" video at 10WordsBook.org.

- What insights did you gain from the video about what it means to be human?
- What insights did you gain about the redefinition of the word *human*?

Definitions and Discussion

Read the two definitions and quotes below. Discuss the contemporary redefinitions of *human* and their cultural consequences.

HUMAN

Pertaining to man (male and female), mankind, humans are physical and spiritual beings, created by God in His image, with intrinsic dignity, incalculable worth, and unalienable rights to life and liberty. Humans are created for an intimate relationship with their Creator, as well as relationships with one another. God created humans to wisely steward and govern the created world, and they are accountable to Him for how they carry out this task.

HUMAN REDEFINED

(1) A form of animal life, the product of a purposeless process of material evolution; a biological machine. (2) A radically autonomous, willing creature. An independent, self-determining agent. (3) A socially and historically determined being, a representative of a particular culture or identity group.

Reflect on these quotes from the *10 Words* book:

"*[There is] no life after death; no ultimate foundation for ethics; no ultimate meaning for life; no free will.*"—William Provine, former Historian of Science and Evolutionary Biology at Cornell University[6]

"A rat is a pig is a dog is a boy."—Ingrid Newkirk, co-founder of PETA (People for the Ethical Treatment of Animals)[7]

"The late modern self would seem to be understood primarily as a self-determining agent whose desires are curbed only by the principle of consent when brought into relationship with the desires of another self-determining agent."—Carl Trueman from The Rise and Triumph of the Modern Self[8]

"It doesn't matter what living, meat skeleton you've been born into; it's what you feel that defines you."—From a BBC The Social YouTube Channel video titled "Boy or Girl?"

"We no longer feel ourselves to be guests in someone else's home and therefore obliged to make our behavior conform with a set of preexisting cosmic rules. It is our creation now. We make the rules. We establish the parameters of reality. We create the world, and because we do, we no longer feel beholden to outside forces. We no longer have to justify our behavior, for we are now the architects of the universe. We are responsible for nothing outside ourselves, for we are the kingdom, the power, and the glory for ever and ever."—Jeremy Rifkin, American Economist and Social Theorist[9]

"Everyone's ideas are . . . merely social constructions stitched together by cultural forces. Individual [people] are little more than mouthpieces for communities based on race, class, gender, ethnicity, and sexual identity."—Nancy Pearcey from Finding Truth[10]

Discussion Questions
- How does the redefinition of *human* differ from the true definition? Discuss all that has changed.
- In what ways have you seen or experienced the various redefinitions of *human*?

- What are some of the social and cultural changes that these redefinitions have resulted in? What kinds of changes in policies and laws?

Personal Reflection and Application
Next week at home, take time to reflect on these areas of application. Read the questions and write down your responses.

Defending human dignity
When deadly lies emerge that dehumanize us, we, as followers of Jesus, must act out of love. We cannot sit back passively or "go along to get along." We must confront the lies and articulate the countervailing and life-affirming truth, helping our neighbors see how the materialistic and postmodern redefinitions of human life that they have believed are reductionist, dehumanizing, and ultimately unlivable. They don't fit who we are or match the real world.

QUESTION: What opportunities has God given you—in your vocation or circle of influence—to confront deadly lies that dehumanize people made in God's image?

Our goal must be to change the hearts and minds of our fellow citizens. We must make crystal clear the vast difference between grubby notions of "human non-persons" and the exalted Christian concept of personhood, which depends not on what I can do but on who I am—that I am created in the image of God. Human beings need not *earn* a standing as creatures of great value. Our dignity is intrinsic, rooted in the fact that God made, knows, and loves us.

The abortion holocaust

Tragically, we are living through perhaps the greatest mass murder of innocent victims in history. Since 1973, when abortion was legalized in all fifty states, more than 63 million innocent unborn human beings have been murdered through abortion in the United States alone. In 2022 the US Supreme Court overturned *Roe V. Wade*, allowing each state to establish laws regarding abortion. Since then, 13 states have banned abortions, and others have restricted them. Yet much remains to be done to protect the most vulnerable among us.

QUESTION: What can you do to support, or further support, the pro-life movement in the United States and around the globe? Many outstanding pro-life organizations exist. What can you do to support their important work?

QUESTION: Abortion has many victims. What can you do to tenderly care for the many victims of abortion, particularly for the countless women whose lives have been shattered? They need to know that forgiveness and loving care are available from Jesus and his church.

In the pro-life movement, there's work for everyone: for artists and musicians, pastors and theologians, statesmen and lawyers, scholars and activists. What role will you play?

Practical care for the most vulnerable

In the end we will be judged by how we cared for the most vulnerable, by how we emulate our heavenly Father: "A father to the fatherless, a defender of the widows, is God in his holy dwelling" (Psalm 68:5); "He will deliver the needy who cry out, the afflicted who have no one to help. He will take pity on the weak and the needy and save the needy from death. He will rescue them from oppression and violence, for precious is their blood in his sight" (Psalm 72:12–14).

Our greatest apologetic as we share God's love will be how we care for weak and vulnerable people made in God's image.

QUESTION: Who are those out of sight and out of mind in your community? The unborn and infant; the elderly and dying; the sick, lonely, and isolated; the sex trafficked; the refugees or aliens? They might be in your home, next door, or down the street.

QUESTION: What practical things can you do to care for and support them and defend their humanity?

Concluding Thoughts

"Above all else, Christianity brought a new conception of humanity to a world saturated with cruelty. What Christianity gave to its converts was nothing less than their humanity."—Rodney Stark[11]

"There are no ordinary people. You have never talked to a mere mortal . . . Next to the Blessed Sacrament itself, your neighbor is the holiest object presented to your senses."—C. S. Lewis from *The Weight of Glory*[12]

RECOMMENDED RESOURCES

Books

- *The Book that Made Your World: How the Bible Created the Soul of Western Civilization* by Vishal Mangalwadi (2012)
- *Dominion: How The Christian Revolution Remade the World* by Tom Holland (2021)
- *The Rise of Christianity: How the Obscure, Marginal Jesus Movement Became the Dominant Religious Force in the Western World in a Few Centuries* by Rodney Stark (1997)
- *Being God's Image: Why Creation Still Matters* by Carmen Joy Imes (2023)
- *The Rise and Triumph of the Modern Self: Cultural Amnesia, Expressive Individualism, and the Road to Sexual Revolution* by Carl R. Trueman (2020)

Videos

- The Bible Project: *You're Supposed to Rule the World (Here's How)* bibleproject.com/explore/video/image-of-god/

SEX

Nothing is more controversial—more contested—in Western culture than issues dealing with sex.

Are we created by God, male and female? Today the most influential voices in the culture answer no. God doesn't determine our gender identity. We do, without any concern for our biology or anatomy.

And gender isn't binary; it's an ever-growing list of explanations, as limitless as the human imagination.

And what about sexual intercourse? That's merely a form of recreation.

But is this true?

What is sex?

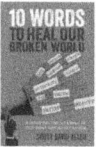

This week we're reading Chapter 3, "Sex," in *10 Words to Heal Our Broken World* by Scott David Allen.

PERSONAL BIBLE STUDY: *SEX*

Before You Begin

In the space below write a concise, dictionary-style definition of the word *sex* from your current understanding without consulting sources such as a dictionary, the internet, or another person. The purpose is to record your current understanding and see how it changes due to this study.

BIBLE STUDY

Read the following passages and prayerfully respond to the question below.

God created mankind in his own image, in the image of God he created them; male and female he created them. (Genesis 1:27)

You [God] created my inmost being; you knit me together in my mother's womb. I praise you because I am fearfully and wonderfully made; your works are wonderful; I know that full well. (Psalm 139:13–14)

QUESTION: What truths do these passages reveal about sex?

Reflect on these quotes from the *10 Words* book:

To understand sex, we begin with truth about the body. Our bodies aren't meaningless matter. They are the handiwork of a loving God. They exhibit order, design, and purpose. Scripture treats body and soul with equal importance as parts of a deeply interconnected whole.

Our sex as male or female is an essential part of our identity. It is not some evolutionary accident. It is a gift we receive, not a choice we make. God expects us to gratefully receive and live in conformity with the body he gave us.

Read the following passages and prayerfully respond to the question below.

"At the beginning the Creator 'made them male and female,' and said, 'For this reason a man will leave his father and mother and be united to his wife, and the two will become one flesh.' So they are no longer two, but one flesh." (Matthew 19:4–6)

Woman is not independent of man, nor is man independent of woman. For as woman came from man, so also man is born of woman. But everything comes from God. (1 Corinthians 11:11–12)

God blessed them and said to them, "Be fruitful and increase in number; fill the earth." (Genesis 1:28)

QUESTION: What truths do these passages further reveal about sex?

Reflect on this quote from the *10 Words* book:

Biologically, physiologically, chromosomally, and anatomically, males and females are counterparts to one another. "To have a male body is to have a body structurally ordered to loving union with a female body, and vice versa,"—Anglican theologian Oliver O'Donovan.[1]

Read the following passages and prayerfully respond to the question below.

Rejoice in the wife of your youth. A loving doe, a graceful deer—may her breasts satisfy you always, may you be intoxicated with her love. (Proverbs 5:18–19)

Let him kiss me with the kisses of his mouth—for your love is more delightful than wine . . . Take me away with you—let us hurry! Let the king bring me into his chambers. (Song of Songs 1:2, 4)

Each man should have sexual relations with his own wife, and each woman with her own husband. The husband should fulfill his marital duty to his wife, and likewise the wife to her husband. The wife does not have authority over her own body but yields it to her husband. In the same way, the husband does not have authority over his own body but yields it to his wife. Do not deprive each other except perhaps by mutual consent and for a time, so that you may devote yourselves to prayer. (1 Corinthians 7:2–5)

QUESTION: What truths do these passages further reveal about sex?

Reflect on these quotes from the *10 Words* book:

"Sex is God's appointed way for two people to say reciprocally to one another, 'I belong completely, permanently, and exclusively to you.'"— Timothy Keller[2]

"Christianity worked a cultural revolution, restraining and channeling . . . eros, elevating the status of both women and of the human body, and infusing marriage—and marital sexuality—with love."—Rod Dreher[3]

Sexual intercourse is not to become an idol. As strange as it may sound in the hypersexualized West, intercourse isn't essential for human flourishing. Jesus is our model of a life perfectly lived. He was a sexed human being with all the longings and desires of any man, yet he was content to be celibate. As Todd Wilson reminds us, "he didn't need sex—not because sex is sinful or was somehow beneath his dignity, but because [sexual intercourse] isn't essential to being human." [4]

Read the following passages and prayerfully respond to the question below.

It is God's will . . . that you should avoid sexual immorality. (1 Thessalonians 4:3)

Flee from sexual immorality. (1 Corinthians 6:18a)

Do you not know that wrongdoers will not inherit the kingdom of God? Do not be deceived: Neither the sexually immoral nor idolaters nor adulterers nor men who have sex with men . . . will inherit the kingdom of God. (1 Corinthians 6:9–10)

Marriage should be honored by all, and the marriage bed kept pure, for God will judge the adulterer and all the sexually immoral. (Hebrews 13:4)

If a man has sexual relations with a man as one does with a woman, both of them have done what is detestable. They are to be put to death. (Leviticus 20:13)

QUESTION: What truths do these passages reveal about sex?

Reflect on these quotes from the *10 Words* book:

Sex isn't restricted to marriage because God is some kind of cosmic killjoy. After all, he designed sex! He knows its life-giving potential. He knows best how to maximize it for human flourishing. Out of his pure love, he graciously warns us of the brokenness that is unleashed when sex is abused.

"Sex isn't a toy or plaything: it's a sacred and sovereign power—strong enough, in fact, to bring new life into being . . . Our sexual capacities are powerful, far too powerful to be used anywhere outside of marriage. They need the safe and stable environment that comes with a 'till death do us part' commitment."[5]

LEARNING TOGETHER: *SEX*
Welcome and Opening Prayer

Opening Discussion
Discuss together what you learned about sex during your personal study. What ideas stood out to you? How did God speak to you through the Scriptures?

Watch the Video and Discuss the Questions Below
Note: You'll find the "sex" video at 10WordsBook.org.
- What insights did you gain from the video about the word *sex*?
- What insights did you gain about the redefinition of sex?

Definitions and Discussion
Read the two definitions and quotes below. Discuss the contemporary redefinition of sex and its cultural consequences.

SEX

(1) The God-created male-female division. (2) Sexual intercourse between a man and a woman; a comprehensive one-flesh union of heart, mind, spirit, and body, often issuing in the gift of children. Sexual intercourse is a gift from God exclusively for the uniting of husband and wife in marriage.

SEX REDEFINED

(1) Synonymous with gender, a social construct; a person's subjective sense of their sexual identity, without regard to biology or anatomy. (2) The ultimate source of personal identity and meaning. (3) Any form of recreational sexual activity done to give pleasure.

Reflect on these quotes from the *10 Words* book:

Sex is just "a piece of body touching another piece of body."—*Alex Morris*[6]

Our culture's gatekeepers believe the Christian sexual ethic is an immoral, harmful, and repressive myth—a means of empowering the despised "patriarchy" to subjugate women.

"Through sex, mankind may attain the great spiritual illumination which will transform the world, which will light up the only path to earthly paradise."—Margaret Sanger, Founder of Planned Parenthood[7]

Human sexuality used to be part of a comprehensive whole that united male and female as husband and wife in a loving, lifetime commitment and bound them to their offspring and to future generations. Today this beautiful sexual mosaic has been shattered. Sex is now separated from marriage, from children, and even from male-female biology.

A tragic consequence of separating sex and procreation is how pregnancy has been devalued and the unborn dehumanized. For many, pregnancy is viewed as a disease and unborn children as a problem to be overcome or, even worse, an enemy to be defeated. The prevention and termination of pregnancy are now described as "essential healthcare" by pro-choice feminists. The abortion genocide is the fruit of this deadly dehumanization of unborn children.

The fruits of the Sexual Revolution have been devastating. We see this in our society's alarmingly high rates of premarital sex, cohabitation, adultery, divorce, out-of-wedlock births, abortion, the hook-up culture, sexual abuse, sex trafficking, sex slavery, the proliferation of pornography and porn addiction . . . and the list goes on.

For postmodernists, the male-female binary is not an objective biological reality but a cultural construction, an oppressive relic of Judeo-Christian morality. Postmodernism holds that the body is a meaningless biological organism. It disconnects the body from the mind, or what it calls the "authentic, choosing self."

The discarding of the male-female sexual binary has given rise to a chaotic proliferation of sexual categories that grows longer with each passing day. In 2016 the New York City Human Rights Commission released a list of 31 terms of gender expression: androgynous, genderqueer, non-binary, pangender, bi-gendered, gender fluid, third sex, two-spirit, *and so on.*

Today, children and youth are then encouraged to "come out" and publicly express their "authentic" gender identity by changing their names, "preferred pronouns," clothes, haircut, voice, and behaviors. An entire industry has developed to facilitate these changes through easy access (often without parental consent) to powerful hormonal drugs and even barbaric sex-reassignment surgeries that frequently render those who undergo them infertile, as well as physically, emotionally, and spiritually traumatized. Everyone else, including the parents of the children, is coerced into affirming and "celebrating" these life-altering choices. "Misgendering," or failure to use someone's preferred pronoun, may lead to your being fired or fined. It may even lead to state officials removing your children from your custody. In several states parents who fail to acknowledge and support their child's gender transition could lose custody rights of their own children to another parent or even the state itself.

Discussion Questions

- How does the redefinition of sex differ from the true definition? Discuss all that has changed.
- In what ways have you seen or experienced the various redefinitions of sex?
- What are some of the social and cultural changes that these redefinitions of sex have resulted in? What kinds of changes have resulted in policies and laws?

Personal Reflection and Application

Next week at home, take time to reflect on these areas of application. Read the questions and write down your responses.

Consider your own understanding.

QUESTION: Based on what you learned in this session, what changes do you need to make in your thinking about the word *sex*?

Consider your own practices

Today many Christians are actively engaged in and even addicted to sexual immorality of one form or another, including pornography, masturbation, premarital sex, adultery, homosexuality, and even pedophilia.

If this describes you, start with confession and repentance. Name your sins specifically and repent. "If we confess our sins, he is faithful and just and will forgive us our sins and purify us from all unrighteousness" (1 John 1:9).

Next, please seek help. Our standard as followers of Jesus Christ must be nothing short of sexual purity. (See 1 Corinthians 6:18 and Colossians 3:5.) But overcoming sexual sin and addictions can't be done alone. We need brothers and sisters in Christ who will hold us accountable. We must lean on the Holy Spirit and prayer.

Defend the truth about sex

Today's gross abuse of sexuality destroys the lives of millions of people and puts them at grave risk of eternal separation from a holy and righteous God. For the revolution's many victims, as well as for the well-being of the church, communities, and nations, we must confront lovingly but firmly the deadly dogmas of the Sexual Revolution.

It isn't loving to either ignore or affirm the abuse of sexuality happening around us. When we bless the relationships God calls sin, we act as though we think ourselves more merciful than God is. We need to speak out. However, how we confront sexual immorality in our culture is critical. Our call is to love our enemies and deal gently with opponents (2 Timothy 2:25). We don't fight as the world fights, with angry and cutting words, threats, and hatred. Rather, we fight with spiritual weapons, with prayer, with the "sword of the Spirit, which is the word of God" (Ephesians 6:17), and in the power of the Holy Spirit.

QUESTION: Considering your vocation and circle of influence, where and how do you need to speak out and defend the truth about sexuality?

If you work in a government agency, school, business, etc., that openly supports the Sexual Revolution and pressures you to affirm what God calls sin, pray for discernment in how to respond. You may need to speak up. If so, do it in prayer and, if possible, with others. Perhaps God will lead you to leave, find a new job, or start a new institution.

Our responsibility as parents

If you are parents of school-aged children, take seriously your responsibility to teach them the truth about sexuality. Take active steps to prevent others from indoctrinating them in sexual sin. You must protect them from threats and false teaching on social media as well as in films, television, and school sex education programs. Do all you can to teach them to love what is good, true, and beautiful, while protecting them from deadly cultural lies.

Concluding Thought

"It is time for evangelicals to rediscover the historic Christian vision of human sexuality. Now, more than at any other time since the first centuries of the church, we need a countercultural Christian sexual ethic and, at an even deeper level, a distinctively Christian view of human sexuality. We need a fresh encounter with what has been called the 'jarring gospel of Christian sexuality' that transformed the pagan world."—Todd Wilson, *Mere Sexuality: Recovering the Christian Vision of Sexuality*[8]

RECOMMENDED RESOURCES

Books

- *The Grand Design: Rediscovering Male and Female as the Image of God* by Darrow L. Miller (2023)
- *Mere Sexuality: Recovering the Christian Vision of Sexuality* by Todd Wilson (2017)
- *Love Thy Body: Answering Hard Questions about Life and Sexuality* by Nancy Pearcey (2018)
- *Strange New World: How Thinkers and Activists Redefined Identity and Sparked the Sexual Revolution* by Carl Trueman (2022)
- *When Harry Became Sally: Responding to the Transgender Moment* by Ryan Anderson (2018)

Film

- *What Is a Woman?* A 2022 documentary film by Matt Walsh available on Daily Wire, dailywire.com/videos/what-is-a-woman.

MARRIAGE

Since the early 2000s the word *marriage* has been at the center of a bitterly fought culture war, and one side has prevailed.

The victors have successfully redefined marriage in the broader culture. It now means something entirely different from what it did as recently as twenty years ago.

In one of the most widely used dictionaries in America, marriage is defined this way:

"Marriage is a legally recognized relationship, established by a civil or religious ceremony, between two people who intend to live together as sexual and domestic partners."

This definition is now enshrined in our laws and taught in our schools. But is this what marriage *really* is?

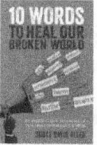 This week we're reading Chapter 4, "Marriage," in *10 Words to Heal Our Broken World* by Scott David Allen.

PERSONAL BIBLE STUDY: *MARRIAGE*

Before You Begin

In the space below write a concise, dictionary-style definition of marriage from your current understanding without consulting sources such as a dictionary, the internet, or another person. The purpose is to record your current understanding and see how it changes due to this study.

BIBLE STUDY

Read the following passages and prayerfully respond to the question below.

The LORD God said, "It is not good for the man to be alone. I will make a helper suitable for him" . . . So the LORD God caused the man to fall into a deep sleep; and while he was sleeping, he took one of the man's ribs and then closed up the place with flesh. Then the LORD God made a woman from the rib he had taken out of the man, and he brought her to the man. The man said, "This is now bone of my bones and flesh of my flesh; she shall be called 'woman,' for she was taken out of man." That is why a man leaves his father and mother and is united to his wife, and they become one flesh. (Genesis 2:18, 21–25)

A man shall leave his father and mother and be united to his wife, and the two will become one flesh. (Ephesians 5:31)

Marriage should be honored by all. (Hebrews 13:4)

He who finds a wife finds what is good and receives favor from the LORD. (Proverbs 18:22)

A wife of noble character who can find? She is worth far more than rubies. (Proverbs 31:10)

QUESTION: What truths do these passages reveal about marriage?

Reflect on these quotes from the *10 Words* book:

Marriage, one of God's greatest gifts to humanity, is a uniquely life-giving, multigenerational, culture-forming, and civilization-building institution. Flourishing societies are built on the foundation of healthy families, which are built on the foundation of strong marriages. Marriage is quite literally the cell of the societal body. What happens in that cell will determine whether the body thrives or dies.

The marriage of Adam and Eve in the Garden of Eden (Genesis 2:18–24), because it happened before the fall, serves as a template for all marriages in all cultures and for all times. Here we see marriage as the exclusive uniting of a man and a woman. Not a man and a man, a woman and a woman, a man and an animal, a man and multiple women, or any other combination. Because God created Adam and Eve male and female, homosexual "marriage" is excluded. Likewise, because Adam could find "no suitable helper" (Genesis 2:20) for himself among the animals, bestiality is excluded. Because God created just one woman for Adam, polygamy is excluded, and the pattern of monogamy is established.

Unity without uniformity and diversity without superiority exists in the godhead. The Father, Son, and Holy Spirit are mysteriously "one" (Deuteronomy 6:4), yet distinct and complementary. Since people are image-bearers of God, this same unity and diversity applies to us. In marriage the husband and wife are profoundly united as "one flesh" (Genesis 2:24), yet they remain distinct. In the relationship between husband and wife, there is unity without uniformity and diversity without superiority.

Read the following passages and prayerfully respond to the question below.

> "For this reason a man will leave his father and mother and be united to his wife, and the two will become one flesh." This is a profound mystery—but I am talking about Christ and the church. (Ephesians 5:31–32)

God has said [to His chosen people, the church], "Never will I leave you; never will I forsake you." (Hebrews 13:5)

I am convinced that [nothing] in all creation will be able to separate us from the love of God that is in Christ Jesus our Lord. (Romans 8:39)

A married woman is bound to her husband as long as he is alive. (Romans 7:2)

Be on your guard, and do not be unfaithful to the wife of your youth. "The man who hates and divorces his wife," says the LORD, the God of Israel, "does violence to the one he should protect," says the LORD Almighty. (Malachi 2:15–16)

To the married I give this command (not I, but the Lord): A wife must not separate from her husband. But if she does, she must remain unmarried or else be reconciled to her husband. And a husband must not divorce his wife. (1 Corinthians 7:10–11)

You shall not commit adultery . . . You shall not covet your neighbor's . . . wife, or his male or female servant. (Exodus 20:14, 17)

"I [Jesus] tell you that anyone who looks at a woman lustfully has already committed adultery with her in his heart." (Matthew 5:28)

"I [Jesus] tell you that anyone who divorces his wife, except for sexual immorality, and marries another woman commits adultery." (Matthew 19:9).

Some Pharisees came and tested [Jesus] by asking, "Is it lawful for a man to divorce his wife?" "What did Moses command you?" he replied. They said, "Moses permitted a man to write a certificate of divorce and send her away." "It was because your hearts were hard that Moses wrote you this law," Jesus replied. "But at the beginning of creation, God 'made them male and female.' 'For this reason, a man will leave his father and mother and be united to his wife, and the two will become one flesh.' So they are no longer two but one flesh. Therefore, what God has joined together, let no one separate." (Mark 10:2–9)

QUESTION: What truths do these passages reveal about the marriage covenant?

Reflect on these quotes from the *10 Words* book:
God designed marriage to be an exclusive, lifelong relationship rooted in a solemn commitment of fidelity. This, too, reflects God's relational nature as a covenant-making, covenant-keeping God. When God makes a covenant with his people, it can never be revoked, even if we fail to uphold our end. As it says in 2 Timothy 2:13, "If we are faithless, he remains faithful, for he cannot deny himself."

In marriage, the husband becomes a living picture of Jesus Christ, who solemnly promises his bride that "neither death nor life, neither angels nor demons, neither the present nor the future, nor any powers, neither height nor depth, nor anything else in all creation, will be able to separate us from the love of God that is in Christ Jesus our Lord" (Romans 8:38–39).

Marriage is a union of heart, mind, spirit, and body. It's not just about the couple's happiness or emotional fulfillment but also about

*children, family, and future generations. It isn't about feeling "in love"
but about fidelity to a lifelong covenant, regardless of the ebb and flow
of emotions. It's a covenant that displays the steadfast love of Christ
for his church.*

**Read the following passages and prayerfully respond to the
question below.**

God blessed [Adam and Eve] and said to them, "Be fruitful
and increase in number; fill the earth." (Genesis 1:28)

Has not the one God made you? You belong to him in body
and spirit. And what does the one God seek? Godly offspring.
(Malachi 2:15a)

Your wife will be like a fruitful vine within your house; your
children will be like olive shoots around your table. Yes, this
will be the blessing for the man who fears the LORD . . . May
you live to see your children's children—peace be on Israel.
(Psalm 128:3–4, 6)

Children are a heritage from the LORD, offspring a reward
from him. Like arrows in the hands of a warrior are children
born in one's youth. Blessed is the man whose quiver is full of
them. (Psalm 127:3–5)

QUESTION: What truths do these passages further reveal about
marriage?

Reflect on these quotes from the *10 Words* book:

Marriage is a relationship like no other because it uniquely involves procreation; raising children; and establishing families, communities, cultures, and nations. Nothing is more miraculous, mysterious, and beautiful than God's partnership with husband and wife in creating a new human being—a unique person of incredible complexity and intricate design, complete with an immortal spirit, mind, and will, with vast potential and incalculable worth. Filling the earth with such people is God's chief purpose in marriage.

"The couple is the starting point, but it's a ripple. It goes around wide. Whatever I do in my marriage, the circle keeps increasing; it keeps widening until it covers the whole world. Marriage is beyond us. It's about society. It's your own project for the world."—Ifeyinwa Awagu[1]

Only one place exists where the power of procreation is both safe and good—within the context of the lifelong covenant of marriage. It is the God-ordained community intended to firmly cement husband to wife and both to the offspring their union produces.

Yet merely having children is not enough; the Lord wants "godly offspring" (Malachi 2:15). To achieve this God designed marriage and the family to be a community of teaching and learning about God and godliness. Both mothers and fathers play vital roles. Proverbs 6:20–21 says: "My son, keep your father's command, and do not forsake your mother's teaching."

Every husband and wife ought to desire a quiver full of well-nurtured "children arrows" to advance God's purposes on earth. As parents mold their children's characters, they, in turn, will influence their children and grandchildren through many generations. "Their children will be mighty in the land; the generation of the upright will be blessed" (Psalm 112:2).

Read the following passages and prayerfully respond to the question below.

> The husband is the head of the wife as Christ is the head of the church, his body, of which he is the Savior. (Ephesians 5:23)

> Husbands, love your wives, just as Christ loved the church and gave himself up for her. (Ephesians 5:25)

> Husbands, love your wives and do not be harsh with them. (Colossians 3:19)

> Husbands ought to love their wives as their own bodies. He who loves his wife loves himself. After all, no one ever hated their own body, but they feed and care for their body, just as Christ does the church. (Ephesians 5:28–29)

> Husbands . . . be considerate as you live with your wives, and treat them with respect as the weaker partner and as heirs with you of the gracious gift of life, so that nothing will hinder your prayers. (1 Peter 3:7)

> Anyone who does not provide for their relatives, and especially for their own household, has denied the faith and is worse than an unbeliever. (1 Timothy 5:8)

QUESTION: What truths do these passages reveal about the husband's role in marriage?

Reflect on these quotes from the *10 Words* book:

The Old Testament word for husband is ishi. This word implies a self-sacrificing, other-serving authority that offers initiative, protection, and provision. The husband's authority in the Bible does not imply his superiority to the wife or their children. Rather, this authority, or headship, involves a willingness to shoulder responsibility and to lovingly serve those under authority. A husband is ultimately responsible for what happens in his household. He must sacrificially serve his wife and children, laying down his prerogatives to attend to their needs, even at the cost of his own life.

"The husband must treat his wife as the most important person in his life other than the Lord. She is his partner, his lover, his best counselor, and his friend. As such, every husband "is under the most solemn obligation to do all in his power to make his wife's life happy, beautiful, noble, and blessed. To do this, he is ready to make any personal sacrifice. Nothing less than this can be implied in loving as Christ loved His Church when He gave himself for it."—J. R. Miller[2]

Read the following passages and prayerfully respond to the question below.

The LORD God said, "It is not good for the man to be alone. I will make a helper suitable for him." (Genesis 2:18)

Wives, submit yourselves to your own husbands as you do to the Lord. For the husband is the head of the wife as Christ is the head of the church, his body, of which he is the Savior. Now as the church submits to Christ, so also wives should submit to their husbands in everything. (Ephesians 5:22–24)

Wives, submit yourselves to your husbands, as is fitting in the Lord. (Colossians 3:18)

The wife must respect her husband. (Ephesians 5:33)

Teach the older women to be reverent in the way they live, not to be slanderers or addicted to much wine, but to teach what is good. Then they can urge the younger women to love their husbands and children, to be self-controlled and pure, to be busy at home, to be kind, and to be subject to their husbands, so that no one will malign the word of God. (Titus 2:2–5)

A wife of noble character who can find? She is worth far more than rubies. Her husband has full confidence in her and lacks nothing of value . . . She is clothed with strength and dignity; she can laugh at the days to come. She speaks with wisdom, and faithful instruction is on her tongue. She watches over the affairs of her household and does not eat the bread of idleness. Her children arise and call her blessed; her husband also, and he praises her: "Many women do noble things, but you surpass them all.: (Proverbs 31:10-11; 25–29)

A wife of noble character is her husband's crown, but a disgraceful wife is like decay in his bones. (Proverbs 12:4)

QUESTION: What truths do these passages reveal about the role of the wife in marriage?

Reflect on these quotes from the *10 Words* book:
God designates Adams' wife by the word ezer, meaning "helper." In Genesis 2:18 God said of Adam, "I will make a helper suitable for him." If God is the archetypal husband, he is also the archetypical

ezer—*helper. "I lift up my eyes to the mountains—where does my help come from? My help comes from the* LORD, *the Maker of heaven and earth" (Psalm 121:1-2). This kind of help doesn't imply weakness or inferiority—far from it! In marriage the husband needs help, and the wife provides it—a picture of true complementarity.*

"Women are not instructed to submit to all men (1 Peter 3:1), but only the wife to her own husband. Submission in marriage should be characterized by a disposition on the part of the wife to follow her husband's authority—an inclination to yield to his leadership. It is an attitude that says: 'I delight for you to take the initiative in our family. I am glad when you take responsibility and lead with love. I don't flourish in the relationship when you are passive, and I have to make sure the family works.'"—John Piper[3]

LEARNING TOGETHER: *MARRIAGE*
Welcome and Opening Prayer

Opening Discussion
Discuss together what you learned about marriage during your personal study. What ideas stood out to you? How did God speak to you through the Scriptures?

Watch the Video and Discuss the Questions Below
Note: You'll find the "marriage" video at 10WordsBook.org.
- What insights did you gain from the video about marriage?
- What insights did you gain about the redefinition of marriage?

Definitions and Discussion
Read together the two definitions and quotes below. Discuss the contemporary redefinition of marriage and its cultural consequences.

MARRIAGE

A God-ordained, comprehensive, exclusive, and permanent union that brings a man and a woman together as husband and wife, to be father and mother to any children their union brings into being. It is based on the anthropological truth that men and women are different and complementary, the biological fact that reproduction depends on a man and a woman, and the social reality that children need both a mother and a father.[4]

MARRIAGE REDEFINED

A legally recognized, romantic caregiving relationship between consenting adults who intend to live together as sexual and domestic partners.

Reflect on these quotes from the *10 Words* book:

Before 1960 and the mainstreaming of the Sexual Revolution, there remained a social stigma associated with sex outside of marriage. Today, by some estimates, a staggering 95 percent of the US population engages in sex outside of marriage, and the notion that sex should be reserved for male-female marriage is viewed as unreasonable, bizarre, and even bigoted.[5]

Before 1960, cohabitation (two unmarried people living together in a sexual relationship) was exceedingly rare and culturally frowned upon. Now cohabitation has become the unquestioned norm. Between 1960 and 2011, cohabitation rates in the United States increased by over 1,000 percent, and the rates are similar in almost all Western nations.[6]

Before 1970 and the advent of no-fault divorce laws, divorce was relatively uncommon and difficult to get. Today, however, about half of all marriages in the United States will end in divorce.[7]

Divorce, cohabitation, and the separation of sex and marriage have led to skyrocketing rates of out-of-wedlock births and all of the accompanying shattered lives and societal disorders. Today, of every 100 children born in the United States, 40 are born to single parents.

With God, procreation, permanence, exclusivity, and covenant all stripped from marriage, the conditions were ripe for the next pillar to fall—the male-female binary. Before 2001 no country, at any time in history, had ever defined marriage as a same-sex institution. In virtually every culture, male and female, sex and procreation had been the beating heart of marriage. But starting with Holland in 2000, 19 countries have officially declared that male and female are no longer essential to marriage. This happened in the United States in 2015 with Obergefell v. Hodges, *in which the Supreme Court redefined marriage for all 50 states.*

Marriage is now an institution exclusively serving the interests of adults. It has been stripped of its intrinsic connection to children, family, or future generations.

Discussion Questions

- How does the redefinition of marriage differ from the true definition? Discuss all that has changed.
- In what ways have you seen or experienced the redefinition of marriage?
- What are some of the social and cultural changes that the redefinition of marriage has resulted in? What kinds of changes have resulted in policies and laws?

Personal Reflection and Application

Next week at home, take time to reflect on these areas of application. Read the questions and write down your responses.

All of us are married, will be married, or know married people. Even if you are single, knowing the truth about marriage is essential.

The broader culture seeks to strip marriage of its meaning, even define it out of existence. We must respond by respectfully standing firm.

Reflect on your thinking about marriage.
QUESTION: What has been most influential in forming your understanding of marriage?

The hard truth is that Bible-believing Christians have tended to think about marriage, sex, birth control, and children in ways that align more with the prevailing culture than with Holy Scripture.

The crying need of the moment is for the church to rediscover the true meaning of marriage and repent of our uncritical acceptance of false cultural values and practices.

Marriage is being destroyed in the West, and Christians must acknowledge our complicity in this. Rather than loving others as Jesus commanded (John 15:12), we have sinned against God and harmed those we are closest to—our husbands, wives, parents, children, or siblings. Too often we have not understood or obeyed God's clear instructions for marriage. But thanks to God, forgiveness is available through Christ. God graciously offers each of us a second chance, a third, or a fourth. "If we confess our sins, he is faithful and just and will forgive us our sins and purify us from all unrighteousness" (1 John 1:9).

Reflect on your thinking about children and family
The prevailing culture values personal autonomy, choice, and materialism, and these values have significantly shaped the views of

marriage for many Christians. Marriage is cast as a loss of personal freedom—a "ball and chain." The good life, we're told, is filled with exciting adventures and material prosperity. Children are said to be a barrier to these goals because they limit freedom and cost a lot of money.

These attitudes are behind the growing trend of young people postponing marriage until their thirties after they're established in the workplace and have secured a bank account large enough to fund their desired standard of living. Add to this mindset readily available, low-cost birth control, a growing hookup culture, and pervasive pornography, and it is little wonder that birth control and abortion are viewed as holy sacraments in the West.

QUESTION: If you are planning on marrying, engaged, or newly married, what are your views on procreation, birth control, and family size? Are they shaped more by contemporary culture or by the Bible?

Christians need wisdom in how we think about birth control. We shouldn't passively accept it as an unquestioned cultural good. We must remember the history behind its creation, development, and unwholesome fruits. While there may be legitimate reasons to limit family size, we dare not take our fears over personal cost or inconvenience as the final word.

Even entertaining the notion that Christians should welcome as many children as God chooses to give is frightening. Most of us feel inadequate to have one child, let alone five, six, or more. And the truth is, in our own strength our fears are well founded. But this is one of the great things about marriage. The whole endeavor is a faith-building exercise, and God is happy to supply our needs as we step out in faith and trust him and his ways.

Reflect on your role as a husband or wife.
QUESTION: If someone were to ask you what the primary role of the husband or wife in marriage is, how would you respond?

QUESTION: If you are a husband or wife, review the passages and quotes from the personal Bible study section that frame the biblical understanding of these roles. What steps can you take to live more obediently to God's design?

Covenant faithfulness
The Bible frames marriage as a living picture of the relationship between Jesus and his Bride, the church. He is utterly faithful to his Bride. He will never leave her or forsake her, and he laid down his life for her. Divorce, adultery, and pornographic usage are all forms of unfaithfulness and covenant-breaking—things that God hates.

QUESTION: How committed are you to covenant faithfulness to your spouse? Do you consider divorce an option when difficult challenges arise in your marriage?

QUESTION: What are your thoughts, behaviors, and habits regarding pornography?

When it comes to pornography, adultery, and divorce, we need to honestly confess our sins—both to God and to our spouse. We must seek to honor God above all and do the necessary work to turn from our sinful habits, thoughts, and behaviors. This is work that requires faithful perseverance. Victory is not easy, but it is possible with God's help and the essential help of trusted fellow Christians who can lovingly support and hold us accountable.

If you are addicted to pornography or are moving in that direction, many excellent organizations and resources exist to help you overcome your addiction. Seek them out. Overcoming these deep addictions is not something you can do in your own strength.

Bearing witness to the truth about marriage in the culture

Beyond our marriages and families, we must courageously bear public witness to the truth about marriage. We need to tell the world that marriage is God's creation and that we are not free to redefine it. Children are a blessing, and they deserve to be raised by the mother and father who gave them birth.

QUESTION: What opportunities or platforms has God given you to defend the truth about marriage? What will you do?

When it comes to marriage, we face a choice. Will we continue to be swept along by destructive cultural currents, or will we be determined to follow God's way, no matter the cost? My prayer is that you will choose to obey God. If you do, then begin, as Joshua did, with this solemn commitment: "As for me and my household, we will serve the LORD" (Joshua 24:15).

Perhaps more than ever before in history, marriage cannot be taken for granted. Success does not happen automatically. It must be passionately pursued.

So, choose this day!

Concluding Thoughts

"Marriage is a union of heart, mind, spirit, and body. It's not just about the couple's happiness or emotional fulfillment but also about children, family, and future generations. It isn't about feeling 'in love' but fidelity to a lifelong covenant, regardless of the ebb and flow of emotions. It's a covenant that displays the steadfast love of Christ for His church."[8]

The dissolution of marriage can be reversed, but only if that reversal begins in the church. Sean McDowell and John Stonestreet are exactly right: "There is no path forward to building a strong marriage culture that does not begin with a revival of God's people to His design for marriage."[9]

The dissolution of marriage, in the final analysis, isn't the work of sexual revolutionaries or LGBTQ+ activists. Our enemy is not flesh and blood. This is clearly Satan's strategy. If he can weaken and destroy marriage and family, he can significantly hinder God's plan to bless the nations. The good news is that this revival has already started. God is leading us there.

RECOMMENDED RESOURCES

- *This Momentary Marriage: A Parable of Permanence* by John Piper (2009)
- *What is Marriage? Man and Women: A Defense* by Sherif Girgis, Ryan T. Anderson, and Robert P. George (2012)
- *Reforming Marriage: Gospel Living for Couples* by Douglas Wilson (2012)
- *Same-Sex Marriage: A Thoughtful Approach to God's Design for Marriage* by John Stonestreet and Sean McDowell (2014)
- *Letters and Papers from Prison* by Dietrich Bonhoeffer, Touchstone; Updated edition (1997)

FREEDOM

Freedom is the ability to do whatever I want, right?

Wrong! In fact, that leads to bondage.

Freedom is fragile. It can thrive only under very specific conditions. Do you know what those conditions are?

Understanding them is essential to preserving freedom and living as a free people.

If we fail to understand, we will inevitably slide into tyranny and bondage.

For the sake of our children and grandchildren, we must not fail. We need to understand freedom accurately.

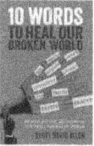

This week we're reading Chapter 5, "Freedom," in *10 Words to Heal Our Broken World* by Scott David Allen.

PERSONAL BIBLE STUDY: *FREEDOM*
Before You Begin
In the space below write a concise, dictionary-style definition of freedom from your current understanding without consulting sources such as a dictionary, the internet, or another person. The purpose is to record your current understanding and see how it changes due to this study.

BIBLE STUDY

Read the following passages and prayerfully respond to the questions below them.

> Our God is in heaven; he does whatever pleases him. (Psalm 115:3)

> With God nothing shall be impossible. (Luke 1:37 KJV)

> [Jesus said,] "The reason my Father loves me is that I lay down my life—only to take it up again. No one takes it from me, but I lay it down of my own accord." (John 10:17–18)

QUESTION: How do these passages reveal God's freedom? Is there anything that limits God's freedom? (hint, see Hebrews 6:18).

> Now the LORD God had planted a garden in the east, in Eden; and there he put the man he had formed. The LORD God made all kinds of trees grow out of the ground—trees that were pleasing to the eye and good for food. In the middle of the garden were the tree of life and the tree of the knowledge of good and evil . . . The LORD God took the man and put him in the Garden of Eden to work it and take care of it. And the LORD God commanded the man, "You are free to eat from any tree in the garden; but you must not eat from the tree of the knowledge of good and evil, for when you eat from it you will certainly die. (Genesis 2:8–9; 15–17)

QUESTION: How does this passage reveal human freedom?

QUESTION: What is the essence of freedom?

QUESTION: Why did God make humans free, with the capacity to make free choices?

Reflect on these quotes from the *10 Words* book:

At the center of freedom are choice and agency. Those fortunate enough to live in relatively free societies experience freedom in their countless daily choices. What will I eat for breakfast? Where will we go on our summer vacation? Where will we attend church? What home or apartment will we live in? What college will I attend? What occupation will I pursue? Who will I vote for to represent my values and preferred policies?

Have you ever wondered why God didn't create us as robots, programmed to respond to him exactly as he wanted? Given our abuse of freedom, that would have saved him a lot of heartache. But as image-bearers of God, we are free because God is free, and he created us with the ability to relate to him as a person, in love. Freedom is essential to this kind of relationship, for love by its very nature must be freely chosen. It can never be compelled or manipulated. Without choice, love makes no sense.

Read the following passages and prayerfully respond to the question below.

[Jesus said,] "Here I am! I stand at the door and knock. If anyone hears my voice and opens the door, I will come in to him and eat with that person, and they with me." (Revelation 3:20)

[Joshua said,] "Choose for yourselves this day whom you will serve . . . as for me and my household, we will serve the LORD." (Joshua 24:15)

"I [God] have set before you life and death, blessings and curses. Now choose life, so that you and your children may live." (Deuteronomy 30:19)

Repent! Turn away from all your offenses; then sin will not be your downfall . . . For I take no pleasure in the death of anyone, declares the Sovereign LORD. Repent and live! (Ezekiel 18:30, 32)

If you declare with your mouth, "Jesus is Lord," and believe in your heart that God raised him from the dead, you will be saved . . . For, "Everyone who calls on the name of the Lord will be saved." (Romans 10:9, 13)

A man reaps what he sows. Whoever sows to please their flesh, from the flesh will reap destruction; whoever sows to please the Spirit, from the Spirit will reap eternal life. (Galatians 6:7–8).

Then I saw a great white throne and him who was seated on it . . . And I saw the dead, great and small, standing before the throne, and books were opened . . . The dead were judged

according to what they had done as recorded in the books
. . . each person was judged according to what they had done.
(Revelation 20:11–13)

QUESTION: What do these passages reveal about human freedom, responsibility, and the consequences of our choices?

Reflect on these quotes from the *10 Words* book:
God has endowed humans with free will, and we are fully responsible for our choices and actions.

God sets before Israel and all of us two paths. One leads to life and freedom under his rule and authority in obedience to his law. The other leads to bondage and destruction through rejecting God and his law. In Deuteronomy 30:19, God says to Israel, "You choose" which path you want and the consequences that will come with that choice.

Read the following passages and prayerfully respond to the questions below.

In their hearts humans plan their course, but the Lord establishes their steps. (Proverbs 16:9)

Come now, you who say, "Today or tomorrow we will go into such and such a town and spend a year there and trade and make a profit"— yet you do not know what tomorrow will bring. What is your life? For you are a mist that appears for a little time and then vanishes. Instead you ought to say, "If the Lord wills, we will live and do this or that." (James 4:13–15 ESV)

[Jesus said,] "You did not choose me, but I chose you and appointed you so that you might go and bear fruit—fruit that will last." (John 15:16)

[God] chose us in him before the creation of the world to be holy and blameless in his sight. In love he predestined us for adoption to sonship through Jesus Christ, in accordance with his pleasure and will. . . In him we were also chosen, having been predestined according to the plan of him who works out everything in conformity with the purpose of his will. (Ephesians 1:4–5, 11)

QUESTION: What do these passages reveal about the relationship between God's sovereignty and human freedom?

QUESTION: Why are human freedom and God's sovereignty both vital to properly understanding reality and to human flourishing?

Reflect on this quote from the *10 Words* book:
The Bible teaches that God is sovereign, all-powerful, and all-knowing. He knows what will happen and guides history toward his chosen ends. Human choices don't constrain him in any way. But are we truly free if we cannot alter God's providential plans by our free choices? Although difficult to understand, the Bible answers in the affirmative. It upholds both God's sovereignty and our freedom. God made us with the capacity

to freely choose, and he holds us accountable and responsible for our moral choices. Yet he works out his sovereign purposes, nonetheless.

Read the following passages and prayerfully respond to the question below.

"You will know the truth, and the truth will set you free." (John 8:32)

I will walk about in freedom, for I have sought out your precepts. (Psalm 119:45)

Live as free people, but do not use your freedom as a cover-up for evil; live as God's slaves. (1 Peter 2:16)

"I have the right to do anything," you say—but not everything is beneficial. "I have the right to do anything"—but I will not be mastered by anything. (1 Corinthians 6:12)

QUESTION: What do these passages reveal about freedom?

Reflect on these quotes from the *10 Words* book:
"God . . . did not create man and then, as an afterthought, impose upon him a set of arbitrary, irritating, restrictive rules. He made man free—and then gave him the Ten Commandments to keep him free . . . We cannot break the Ten Commandments. We can only break ourselves against them—or else, by keeping them, rise through them to the fullness of freedom under God."—Cecil B. DeMille.

Freedom is possible only when citizens are capable of virtuous self-government. In the words of Robert Charles Winthrop (1809–1884), former speaker of the US House of Representatives, "Men must necessarily be controlled, either by a power within them, or by a power without them; either by the word of God, or by the strong arm of man; either by the Bible, or by the bayonet."[1] *It is only through an internally imposed order, or what the Bible calls "self-control" based on God's moral standard, that true freedom exists.*

"Only a virtuous people are capable of freedom . . . As nations become corrupt and vicious they have more need of masters."—Benjamin Franklin

"[I]t is religion and morality alone which can establish the principles upon which freedom can securely stand."—John Adams

"Human nature is constituted by limits, and true freedom is found in the recognition, not the imagined transcendence of, such limits."—Bradford Littlejohn[2]

Read the following passages and prayerfully respond to the question below.

[Jesus said,] "Very truly I tell you, everyone who sins is a slave to sin." (John 8:34)

I am unspiritual, sold as a slave to sin . . . I have the desire to do what is good, but I cannot carry it out. For I do not do the good I want to do, but the evil I do not want to do—this I keep on doing . . . What a wretched man I am! Who will rescue me from this body that is subject to death? (Romans 7:14, 18–19, 24)

Each person is tempted when they are dragged away by their own evil desire and enticed. Then, after desire has conceived, it gives birth to sin; and sin, when it is full-grown, gives birth to death. (James 1:14–16)

QUESTION: What is the relationship between sin (willful disobedience or rebellion against God) and slavery?

Reflect on these quotes from the *10 Words* book:

"It is ordained in the eternal constitution of things, that men of intemperate minds cannot be free. Their passions forge their fetters."— Edmund Burke[3]

We've all felt trapped by various addictions, desires, and compulsions. Trapped by our own hatred and bitterness. We see how they have power over us, holding us captive and leading to the destruction of our lives and relationships. We may deeply desire to be free from the power they wield over us but cannot do so in our own strength. We are under Satan's grip, enslaved by him and destined for destruction. Unless we can be free from this inward bondage, we can never be free people or free citizens in a free society. Internal, spiritual freedom is the foundation of all other freedoms.

Read the following passages and prayerfully respond to the questions below.

Where the Spirit of the Lord is, there is freedom. (2 Corinthians 3:17)

Through Christ Jesus the law of the Spirit who gives life has set you free from the law of sin and death. (Romans 8:2)

We know that our old self was crucified with [Jesus] so that the body ruled by sin might be done away with, that we should no longer be slaves to sin— because anyone who has died has been set free from sin . . . But thanks be to God that, though you used to be slaves to sin . . . you have been set free from sin and have become slaves to righteousness. (Romans 6:6–7, 17–18)

You are no longer a slave, but God's child; and since you are his child, God has made you also an heir. (Galatians 4:7)

It is for freedom that Christ has set us free. Stand firm, then, and do not let yourselves be burdened again by a yoke of slavery. (Galatians 5:1)

[Jesus] shared in their humanity so that by his death he might break the power of him who holds the power of death—that is, the devil—and free those who all their lives were held in slavery by their fear of death. (Hebrews 2:14–15)

[Jesus said,] "If the Son sets you free, you will be free indeed." (John 8:36)

You, my brothers and sisters, were called to be free. But do not use your freedom to indulge the flesh; rather, serve one another humbly in love. (Galatians 5:13)

QUESTION: What do these passages reveal about Jesus, our liberator? How did he free us? From what have we been freed?

QUESTION: According to Galatians 5:13, what is the ultimate purpose of freedom?

Reflect on these quotes from the *10 Words* **book:**

As God's beloved children, we are no longer enslaved by Satan. We have been ransomed, our souls have been purchased at the price of Christ's blood on the cross. Because Jesus died, was buried, and rose again to new life, we, too, have died to our old, sinful nature and are remade. We have been given a new heart and Spirit and the power to obey God and do what pleases him. God, in Christ, has given us new power to be virtuous, self-governing people—free people.

The movement from slavery to freedom is a central theme in the Bible, and the dramatic story of the Jewish exodus from Egypt foreshadows the coming of Jesus, the Messiah, who would make a way for the world to be set free from its enslavement to Satan.

Through faith in Christ, we increasingly bear the "fruit" of the Spirit: love; joy; peace; patience; kindness; goodness; faithfulness; gentleness; and, last but not least, self-control, the supreme virtue needed to sustain freedom.

Read the following passage and quotes from the *10 Words* **book and prayerfully respond to the question below.**

Proclaim liberty throughout the land to all its inhabitants (Leviticus 25:10).

Historically, free nations are not the norm. The default in our fallen world is totalitarianism and empire, where powerful oligarchs and tyrants selfishly exploit the powerless, and personal freedom is non-existent.

Without God, there is no moral law or objective good or evil. In the secular-materialist Darwinian worldview, the only "law" is survival of the fittest. If the powerful are inclined to strip you of your freedom and enslave you for their benefit, what's to stop them?

As Northern European peoples began to read the Bible in their heart languages after the Reformation, they discovered principles that gave rise not to political tyrannies but to free nations in the pattern of ancient Israel. They began to develop a theology of free, self-governing nations where the law was king and human law was legitimate only when grounded in God's moral law. Where powerful rulers were subject to the same laws as everyone else. Where serfs, peasants, and slaves were elevated to the position of free citizens who had the authority to self-govern under God's law. Where civil authorities became "civil servants" and were made accountable to citizens.

There is a reason that free nations emerged in the Christian West following the Reformation—and nowhere else.

We possess freedom as a gift from God. To their everlasting credit, America's Founding Fathers acknowledged this powerful truth in the Declaration of Independence. "We hold these truths to be self-evident, that all men are created equal, that they are endowed by their Creator with certain unalienable Rights, that among these are Life, *Liberty* and the pursuit of Happiness" (emphasis added).

"Christianity, and nothing else, is the ultimate foundation of liberty, conscience, human rights, and democracy, the benchmarks of Western civilization. To this day, we have no other options [than Christianity]. We continue to nourish ourselves from this source. Everything else is postmodern chatter."—Jürgen Habermas[4]

QUESTION: In your own words, why was biblical Christianity essential for the rise of free nations?

LEARNING TOGETHER: *FREEDOM*

Welcome and Opening Prayer

Opening Discussion

Discuss together what you learned about freedom during your personal study. What ideas stood out to you? How did God speak to you through the Scriptures?

Watch the Video and Discuss the Questions Below
Note: You'll find the "freedom" video at 10WordsBook.org.

- What insights did you gain from the video about freedom?
- What insights did you gain about the redefinition of freedom?

Definitions and Discussion

Read the two definitions and quotes below. Discuss the contemporary redefinition of freedom and its cultural consequences.

FREEDOM

The capacity to self-govern; to act according to one's choices within God's created order and under His moral law.

FREEDOM REDEFINED

The power or right to act, speak or think as one wants without hindrance or restraint.[5]

Reflect on these quotes from the *10 Words* book:

Today, freedom means the right to do whatever you want, so long as it doesn't harm anyone else.

Redefined freedom rests on the assumption that humans are sovereign, autonomous individuals, no longer part of God's creation and under his law. We are a law unto ourselves. In the words of US Supreme Court Justice Anthony Kennedy in his majority opinion in the 1992 Planned Parenthood v. Casey *decision: "At the heart of liberty is the right to define one's own concept of existence, of meaning, of the universe, and of the mystery of human life."*[6]

*"We have embarked on a strange and perilous project: to transform ourselves into entirely new creatures, not bound by the rules of mortal, biological life or by the God who created us. We have no gender but what we choose, no morals but those we embrace, no debt that we owe to the future in repayment for all the gifts [we've received] from the past. Our "choices" are sacrosanct and beyond any criticism."—*John Zmirak[7]

Redefined freedom replaces virtue with "If it feels good, do it" and self-control with self-indulgence. The results? On the personal level, ever-growing bondage to the flesh, appetites, and desires, along with unprecedented levels of depression, mental illness, and suicide. At the societal level, skyrocketing rates of drug addiction, soaring crime rates, family breakdown, and increasing social chaos. The social fabric is unraveling. The anti-Christian worldview at the center is incapable of holding a free society together.

Today, many promote the value of "equity," which means equality of outcome. However, any ideology whose primary goal is "equality of outcome" is, by its very nature, anti-freedom. It requires heavy-handed, top-down social engineering. People's choices are respected in free nations, although they invariably lead to different outcomes.

Christianity recognized essential truths that gave rise to free people and free nations. We are now living through a social experiment to see if freedom can be sustained once these truths are rejected, and the answer seems to be negative.

"Freedom is being destroyed primarily by those who scorn the idea that freedom comes from God . . . Wherever God is delinked from freedom, freedom ultimately withers. When Christianity died in Europe, it was replaced by fascism, Nazism, and communism."—Paul Kingsnorth[8]

Discussion Questions

- How does the redefinition of freedom differ from the true definition? Discuss all that has changed.
- In what ways have you seen or experienced the redefinitions of freedom?
- What are some of the social and cultural changes that the redefinition of freedom has resulted in? What kinds of changes have taken place in policies and laws?

Personal Reflection and Application

Next week at home, take time to reflect on these areas of application. Read the questions and write down your responses.

Freedom is a core characteristic of God's kingdom. However, freedom is also fragile and can flourish only under particular conditions. Because freedom is deeply rooted in the Judeo-Christian worldview, the recovery of freedom must be championed, first and foremost, by God-fearing Jews and by followers of Jesus Christ. We are stewards of the truth, not for ourselves but for the nations we are called to disciple and to bless.

Your own understanding

QUESTION: How has this session impacted your understanding of freedom? How do you need to think and act differently?

Freedom requires self-control

To live as a free human being, we must self-govern within God's created order and law. Christ has set us free from slavery to sin and Satan, but we must actively walk in that freedom, or we can slide into bondage again. We live as free, responsible people by turning from sin, controlling ourselves, and doing what is good and pleasing to God. Self-control is a fruit of the Holy Spirit but also a discipline that must be practiced.

QUESTION: In what areas of your life do you need to exercise greater self-control?

QUESTION: Are there any habits or addictions that continue to have control over you and keep you in bondage? What steps will you take to overcome that bondage?

We all struggle with various bondages and addictions. To overcome them, the first step is to transparently confess them to God, receive his gracious forgiveness, and then commit to walking in his liberating strength to overcome bondage. God made you to be free. Jesus died to secure your freedom. Seek to honor him above all; he will help you live in freedom.

Self-control is learned in the home
Self-control is a virtue best learned at home, with Christian parents serving as role models. Christian schools and churches can support parents by inculcating virtue in children and young adults.

QUESTION: If you are a parent of school-aged children, what can you do to raise them to be God-fearing, virtuous, honest, hardworking, self-governing adults capable of living free?

Defending freedom and resisting tyranny
The enemies of Christ call true freedom tyranny, for what they desire above all else is to live in a world without limits, particularly on matters of sexuality. But that world doesn't exist, and any attempt to live as if it does will end in disaster. We must call people back to true freedom and what it takes to sustain it. That necessarily includes freedom in Christ.

Many non-believers are ready to hear this message. They see the growing threats to freedom in our country and around the world—threats to our freedom of speech and our freedom of religion, among others. They, too, love freedom and don't want their children and grandchildren to live under a dictatorship. But they don't know how to turn things around. Let's be ready to answer them and show them.

First, they need to know that secularism cannot sustain free nations. Only a biblical worldview supplies the truths and first principles necessary for free nations. These have to be clearly understood, carefully articulated, and courageously defended. As followers of Jesus, we have work to do.

QUESTION: What opportunities do you have to teach others about true freedom and defend it in the public arena?

QUESTION: What can you do to defend our most basic freedoms that are increasingly under attack, particularly free speech and freedom of religion?

A simple way to do this is to support freedom advocacy organizations such as the Alliance Defending Freedom and others that provide legal defense to those under attack. You can also support businesses and organizations that are pro-freedom, not those that actively work to curtail personal freedoms.

But more than anything else, we have to choose to live as free people and refuse to bow to would-be dictators and their tyrannical designs. Freedom is fragile. It must be defended by each generation, now more than ever.

Concluding Thoughts

"Freedom is a need of the soul. Without freedom, the soul dies. God alone is the inciter and guarantor of freedom. He is the only guarantor. External freedom is only an aspect of interior freedom. Political freedom, as the Western world has known it, is only a political reading of the Bible."—Whittaker Chambers[9]

"Freedom is never more than one generation away from extinction . . . It must be fought for, protected, and handed on for [our children] to do the same, or one day, we will spend our sunset years telling our children and our children's children what it was once like in the United States where men were free."—Ronald Reagan[10]

RECOMMENDED RESOURCES

- *A Free People's Suicide: Sustainable Freedom and the American Future* by Os Guinness (2012)
- *Last Call for Liberty: How America's Genius for Freedom Has Become Its Greatest Threat* by Os Guinness (2018)
- *The Magna Carta of Humanity: Sinai's Revolutionary Faith and the Future of Freedom* by Os Guinness (2021)
- *If You Can Keep It: The Forgotten Promise of American Liberty* by Eric Metaxas (2017)
- *The History of Religious Liberty: From Tyndale to Madison* by Michael Farris (2015)
- *Free Indeed: Living Life in Light of the Biblical View of Freedom* by Art Lindsley (2016)
- *While Time Remains: A North Korean Defector's Search for Freedom in America* by Yeonmi Park (2024)
- *The Indispensable Right: Free Speech in an Age of Rage* by Jonathan Turley (2024)

AUTHORITY

For many people the word *authority* is almost entirely negative. It conjures up images of powerful, dangerous, and unaccountable people who are called "authoritarians."

We are taught to mistrust authority and question it. The idea of submission to authority is equally repulsive.

There's a reason for this.

In our fallen world, authority is often abused, and most of us have been wounded by those in authority in our families or places of work.

But before we dismiss authority entirely, let's ask ourselves, Do we know what true authority is? What does it look like?

 This week we're reading Chapter 6, "Authority," in *10 Words to Heal Our Broken World* by Scott David Allen.

PERSONAL BIBLE STUDY: *AUTHORITY*

Before You Begin

In the space below write a concise, dictionary-style definition of authority from your current understanding without consulting sources such as a dictionary, the internet, or another person. The purpose is to record your current understanding and see how it changes due to this study.

BIBLE STUDY

Read the following passages and prayerfully respond to the question below.

> [Jesus] got up and rebuked the winds and the waves, and it was completely calm. The [disciples] were amazed and asked, "What kind of man is this? Even the winds and the waves obey him!" (Matthew 8:26–27)

> When Jesus had entered Capernaum, a centurion came to him, asking for help. "Lord," he said, "my servant lies at home paralyzed, suffering terribly."
> Jesus said to him, "Shall I come and heal him?"
> The centurion replied, "Lord, I do not deserve to have you come under my roof. But just say the word, and my servant will be healed. For I myself am a man under authority, with soldiers under me. I tell this one, 'Go,' and he goes; and that one, 'Come,' and he comes. I say to my servant, 'Do this,' and he does it."
> When Jesus heard this, he was amazed and said to those following him, "Truly I tell you, I have not found anyone in Israel with such great faith." (Matthew 8:5–10)

> For the LORD is our judge, the LORD is our lawgiver, the LORD is our king. (Isaiah 33:22)

QUESTION: What do these passages reveal about authority and what it means to have authority?

Reflect on this quote from the *10 Words* book:
Webster's 1828 Dictionary of the English Language defines authority as "legal power, or a right to command . . . The power of him whose will and commands must be submitted to by others and obeyed." Think of a judge who issues binding rulings. Or the authority of parents to command, direct, and discipline their children in the home, or the authority of teachers to direct and discipline their students in the classroom.

Read the following passages and prayerfully respond to the question below.

The LORD has established his throne in heaven, and his kingdom rules over all. (Psalm 103:19)

The LORD Most High is awesome, the great King over all the earth. (Psalm 47:2)

Job replied to the LORD: "I know that you can do all things; no purpose of yours can be thwarted." (Job 42:1–2)

And God spoke all these words: "I am the LORD your God, who brought you out of Egypt, out of the land of slavery. You shall have no other gods before me." (Exodus 20:1–3)

The high priest asked [Jesus], "Are you the Messiah, the Son of the Blessed One?"

"I am," said Jesus. "And you will see the Son of Man sitting at the right hand of the Mighty One and coming on the clouds of heaven." (Mark 14:61–62)

Jesus came to [His disciples] and said, "All authority in heaven and on earth has been given to me." (Matthew 28:18)

God [The Father] exalted [Jesus] to the highest place and gave him the name that is above every name, that at the name of Jesus every knee should bow, in heaven and on earth and under the earth, and every tongue acknowledge that Jesus Christ is Lord, to the glory of God the Father. (Philippians 2:9–11)

In [Jesus] all things were created: things in heaven and on earth, visible and invisible, whether thrones or powers or rulers or authorities; all things have been created through him and for him. He is before all things, and in him all things hold together. (Colossians 1:16–17)

QUESTION: What do these passages reveal about the authority of God the Father and God the Son?

Reflect on this quote from the *10 Words* book:
There is no more basic or important truth than this: God is the supreme authority. He "has established his throne in heaven, and his kingdom rules over all" (Psalm 103:19). He is the supreme authority, "the great King over all the earth" (Psalm 47:2).

Read the following passages and prayerfully respond to the question below.

Your word, LORD, is eternal; it stands firm in the heavens. (Psalm 119:89)

As the rain and the snow come down from heaven, and do not return to it without watering the earth and making it bud and flourish, so that it yields seed for the sower and bread for the eater, so is my word that goes out from my mouth: It will not return to me empty, but will accomplish what I desire and achieve the purpose for which I sent it. (Isaiah 55:10–11)

The grass withers and the flowers fall, but the word of our God endures forever. (Isaiah 40:8)

Do not add to what I [God] command you and do not subtract from it, but keep the commands of the LORD your God that I give you (Deuteronomy 4:2).

All Scripture is God-breathed and is useful for teaching, rebuking, correcting and training in righteousness. (2 Timothy 3:16)

QUESTION: What do these passages reveal about the authority of God's Word in Scripture?

Reflect on this quote from the *10 Words* book:
The etymology of the English word authority goes back to the old French word autorite, *meaning an "authoritative book, or the Scriptures." The Reformers emphasized this in one of their famous "solas," Sola Scriptura," or Scripture Alone. God's Word, the Bible, is the highest in authority and must be obeyed above all earthly authorities.*

Read the following passages and prayerfully respond to the question below.

Then God said, "Let us make mankind in our image, in our likeness, so that they may rule over the fish in the sea and the birds in the sky, over the livestock and all the wild animals,

and over all the creatures that move along the ground."
(Genesis 1:26)

You [God] have made [mankind] a little lower than the angels
and crowned them with glory and honor. You made them
rulers over the works of your hands; you put everything under
their feet: all flocks and herds, and the animals of the wild, the
birds in the sky, and the fish in the sea, all that swim the paths
of the seas. (Psalm 8:5–8)

There is no authority except that which God has established.
The [human] authorities that exist have been established by
God. (Romans 13:1)

"Do you refuse to speak to me?" Pilate said. "Don't you realize
I have power [authority] either to free you or to crucify you?"
Jesus answered, "You would have no power over me if it
were not given to you from above." (John 19:10–11)

QUESTION: What do these passages reveal about human authority
and its source?

Reflect on these quotes from the *10 Words* book:
*At creation, God establishes a basic hierarchy of authority. God (and
His Word in Scripture) is the supreme authority. Human beings are
subordinate to God in the creational hierarchy, but they are endowed
with authority over themselves and the rest of creation. Our positions
of authority are God granted, and we are responsible and accountable
to God for exercising our authority. It is a trust. A form of stewardship.*

God delegates or shares his authority with people and establishes the pattern of people sharing authority with other humans to effect change. God delegates authority, for example, to parents regarding the education and upbringing of their children or to elders regarding leadership in a local church. Or think of Moses delegating authority to judge disputes to lower authorities accountable to him (Exodus 18:13–26).

Read the following passages and prayerfully respond to the question below.

I discipline my body and keep it under control. (1 Corinthians 9:27 ESV)

Make every effort to supplement your faith with . . . self-control. (2 Peter 1:5–6)

Wives, submit yourselves to your own husbands as you do to the Lord. For the husband is the head of the wife as Christ is the head of the church, his body, of which he is the Savior. Now as the church submits to Christ, so also wives should submit to their husbands in everything. (Ephesians 5:22–24)

Children, obey your parents in the Lord, for this is right. "Honor your father and mother"—which is the first commandment with a promise—"so that it may go well with you and that you may enjoy long life on the earth." (Ephesians 6:1–3)

Let everyone be subject to the governing authorities . . . This is also why you pay taxes, for the authorities are God's servants, who give their full time to governing. Give to everyone what you owe them: If you owe taxes, pay taxes; if revenue, then revenue; if respect, then respect; if honor, then honor. (Romans 13:1, 6–7)

To the elders among you, I appeal as a fellow elder and a witness of Christ's sufferings who also will share in the glory to be revealed: Be shepherds of God's flock that is under your care, watching over them—not because you must, but because you are willing, as God wants you to be; not pursuing dishonest gain, but eager to serve; not lording it over those entrusted to you, but being examples to the flock. (1 Peter 5:1–3)

Remember your [spiritual] leaders, who spoke the word of God to you. Consider the outcome of their way of life and imitate their faith . . . Have confidence in your leaders and submit to their authority, because they keep watch over you as those who must give an account. (Hebrews 13:7, 17)

QUESTION: Based on these Scriptures, describe four "spheres" of authority God establishes in the Scripture. What is the sphere, and who has authority?

Reflect on these quotes from the *10 Words* book:

Authority over self is referred to in the Bible as "self-control." Self-control is another way of saying "self-government" or authority over one's thoughts and actions. We have the God-given capacity to self-govern, to make choices, and to determine courses of action under God's ultimate authority. In this we differ from the rest of the animal kingdom. Animals, such as pets or livestock, do not govern themselves but are governed by instinct or by people. Because God grants us authority to self-govern, no person has a right to enslave others or take away their authority to self-govern.

God has established roles of human authority. These include husbands in marriage, parents in the home, elders in the local church, and civil authorities in the state. Others include teachers in their classrooms and rightful authorities in businesses or organizations. Authority over other human beings is always temporary. Parents have authority over their children only while under their direct supervision at home. Supervisors in the workplace have authority over their subordinates only as long as they hold their position of authority, and so on. Authority is not an innate, permanent role reserved for elite people. It is a temporary role, something for all of us. But it is a skill and a responsibility we must learn to exercise rightly.

Our submission to legitimate human authorities is an act of obedience to God because he establishes human authority, which is accountable to him for its proper exercise. However, just because authorities have been established by God does not mean that they will exercise authority in God-honoring ways. In a fallen world, rightful authorities often abuse authority for selfish ends, and there certainly are circumstances when disobedience to abusive, illegitimate authority is necessary. However, disobedience to authorities should be the exception, not the rule, and should be undertaken only after careful prayer and discernment. Our default setting should be respectful submission to rightful human authorities "out of reverence for Christ" (Ephesians 5:21).

Read the following passages and prayerfully respond to the question below.

Jesus called [the disciples] together and said, "You know that those who are regarded as rulers of the Gentiles lord it over them, and their high officials exercise authority over them. Not so with you. Instead, whoever wants to become great among you must be your servant, and whoever wants to be first must be slave of all. For even the Son of Man did not come to be served, but to serve, and to give his life as a ransom for many." (Mark 10:42–45)

Jesus knew that the Father had put all things under his power, and that he had come from God and was returning to God; so he got up from the meal, took off his outer clothing, and wrapped a towel around his waist. After that, he poured water into a basin and began to wash his disciples' feet, drying them with the towel that was wrapped around him . . . When he had finished washing their feet, he put on his clothes and returned to his place. "Do you understand what I have done for you?" he asked them. "You call me 'Teacher' and 'Lord,' and rightly so, for that is what I am. Now that I, your Lord and Teacher, have washed your feet, you also should wash one another's feet. I have set you an example that you should do as I have done for you." (John 13:3–5, 12–15)

Rulers hold no terror for those who do right, but for those who do wrong. Do you want to be free from fear of the one in authority? Then do what is right and you will be commended. For the one in authority is God's servant for your good. But if you do wrong, be afraid, for rulers do not bear the sword for no reason. They are God's servants, agents of wrath to bring punishment on the wrongdoer. (Romans 13:3–4)

Husbands, love your wives, just as Christ loved the church and gave himself up for her. (Ephesians 5:25)

Husbands, love your wives and do not be harsh with them. (Colossians 3:19)

Fathers, do not exasperate your children; instead, bring them up in the training and instruction of the Lord. (Ephesians 6:4)

Masters, provide your [servants] with what is right and fair, because you know that you also have a Master in heaven. (Colossians 4:1)

QUESTION: How are those in positions of authority to exercise authority? What does true authority look like in practice?

Reflect on these quotes from the *10 Words* book:

Jesus provides the most striking model for true authority. Though King of kings, he was born in the humblest of settings, in a barn, in a rural backwater, far from the centers of earthly power. His parents were simple laborers with no formal education. From Jesus we learn that authority need not be accompanied by wealth, prestige, or elite status. He taught his followers that the defining characteristic of true authority is humble, sacrificial service. He didn't lord his authority over his followers but treated them as friends (John 15:15). He washed their feet (John 13:4–5) and eventually sacrificed his life so they might live (John 15:13).

Genuine authority is a form of service to those under authority for their own good. Families, communities, businesses, churches, sports teams, and nations thrive where authority's boundaries are respected. True authority supports freedom and maximizes creativity, innovation, and prosperity. It creates environments where people are free to rise to their potential.

Read the following passage and quotes from the *10 Words* book and prayerfully respond to the question below.

God created mankind in his own image, in the image of God he created them; male and female he created them. (Genesis 1:27)

In Christ Jesus you are all children of God through faith, for all of you who were baptized into Christ have clothed yourselves with Christ. There is neither Jew nor Gentile, neither slave nor free, nor is there male and female, for you are all one in Christ Jesus. (Galatians 3:26–28)

Submit to one another out of reverence for Christ. (Ephesians 5:21)

The entire law is fulfilled in keeping this one command: "Love your neighbor as yourself." (Galatians 5:14)

I [Paul] appeal to you [Philemon] for my son Onesimus [Philemon's runaway slave], who became my son while I was in chains . . . Perhaps the reason he was separated from you for a little while was that you might have him back forever—no longer as a slave, but better than a slave, as a dear brother. He is very dear to me . . . both as a fellow man and as a brother in the Lord. (Philemon 10,15–16)

QUESTION: What is the relationship among human equality, human dignity, and the responsibilities of authority and submission?

Reflect on this quote from the *10 Words* book:

As image-bearers of God, human beings also have equality of essence alongside roles of authority and subordination. Our equality of essence comes from God having created us in his divine image. Therefore, we have equal worth. Our basic relationship with other human beings is one of fundamental equality. There are no inherently superior or inferior people. Yet this does not foreclose roles of authority or systems of hierarchy. At different times each of us exercises and submits to authority, often simultaneously. But we should always remember, regardless of our position or role, that human beings are equal in God's sight. Equally valued. Equally loved. True authority, properly exercised, recognizes this fundamental truth and treats all people with equal dignity as God's beloved image-bearers.

Read the following passages and prayerfully respond to the question below.

The king of Egypt said to the Hebrew midwives, whose names were Shiphrah and Puah, "When you are helping the Hebrew women during childbirth on the delivery stool, if you see that the baby is a boy, kill him; but if it is a girl, let her live." The midwives, however, feared God and did not do what the king of Egypt had told them to do; they let the boys live. (Exodus 1:15–17)

"Now when you hear the sound of the . . . music, if you are ready to fall down and worship the image I made, very good. But if you do not worship it, you will be thrown immediately into a blazing furnace. Then what god will be able to rescue you from my hand?"

Shadrach, Meshach and Abednego replied to him, "King Nebuchadnezzar, we do not need to defend ourselves before you in this matter. If we are thrown into the blazing furnace, the God we serve is able to deliver us from it, and he will deliver us from Your Majesty's hand. But even if he does not, we want you to know, Your Majesty, that we will not serve your gods or worship the image of gold you have set up." (Daniel 3:15–18)

"We [the Jewish religious leaders] gave you [Peter and the apostles] strict orders not to teach in [Jesus's] name," Peter said. "Yet you have filled Jerusalem with your teaching and are determined to make us guilty of this man's blood."

Peter and the other apostles replied: "We must obey God rather than human beings!" (Acts 5:28–29)

QUESTION: Based on these verses, when is it proper to disobey those in positions of authority?

Reflect on this quote from the *10 Words* book:

Legitimate authority is limited to doing what is good for those under authority, and good is defined by God's character and his moral law. Authority used to compel what is immoral or evil is illegitimate. For example, civil authorities in the Nazi regime in the 1930s promulgated laws that forbade German citizens from providing aid to Jews. Violators were shipped off to concentration camps. Because this manmade law contradicted God's moral law, which forbids murder (Exodus 20:13), it is both evil and illegitimate. German citizens had a moral duty to disobey it.

LEARNING TOGETHER: *AUTHORITY*
Welcome and Opening Prayer

Opening Discussion

Discuss together what you learned about authority during your personal study. What ideas stood out to you? How did God speak to you through the Scriptures?

Watch the Video and Discuss the Questions Below

Note: You'll find the "authority" video at 10WordsBook.org.

- What insights did you gain from the video about authority?
- What insights did you gain about the redefinition of authority?

Definitions and Discussion

Read the two definitions below. Discuss the contemporary redefinition of authority and its cultural consequences.

AUTHORITY

The power or right to issue commands, rules, or laws and to ensure they are carried out. Human authority is delegated from God, the supreme authority, and is accountable to Him. When properly exercised, authority creates conditions in which people thrive by providing wise leadership in a context of ordered liberty. Jesus, our model for authority in practice, sacrificially serves those under authority for their good.

AUTHORITY REDEFINED

An arbitrary, self-serving, and often harsh and oppressive use of power and control. A concentration of power in human government or rule that is unaccountable to God, constitutional limits, or the people under authority.

Reflect on these quotes from the *10 Words* book:

False authorities exercise their power and control in oppressive ways, as Jesus said, "lording it over" subordinates (Matthew 20:25), who are reduced to little more than serfs, peasants, or slaves.

J. R. R. Tolkien portrayed this false authority as the "one ring" in his grand epic trilogy The Lord of the Rings. False authority is simply the exercise of raw power, with all of true authority's positive, constructive elements stripped away.

False authority creates a stifling, controlled order maintained by fear and threats. It rejects the inherent right to liberty that image-bearers of God possess. "Ordered liberty" is nowhere in sight. There is no basis for liberty at all. Whenever fallen authority is exercised, freedom dies. The order that results from false authority is the order of the gulag.

False authority treats those in power as inherently superior and those in submission as inferior. The concept of submission becomes entirely negative. Because false authority is so common, even Christians reject the concept of submission, particularly in the areas of church, marriage, and family.

Authority stripped of God has no place for decentralized or delegated authority. Rather, power becomes centralized, top-down, and tyrannical. Authority is granted to whoever can grasp the "ring of power" and force others to submit to their authority.

False authority has none of the limits of true authority. The concept of God-ordained spheres of authority is entirely absent. As a result, the authority of people to self-govern, the authority of parents in the home, or the authority of elders in the church are increasingly violated or usurped by secular civil authorities, who view these competing spheres as a threat to their ultimate power.

Postmodernism's grounding of authority in the autonomous individual is unsustainable. Society has to be ordered, and institutions must be established based on somebody's view of reality. The question is, whose? The answer is whoever can amass the power to impose his or her view on everyone else. Postmodernism's radical autonomy is giving way to tyranny by powerful ruling elites who displace God at the top of the hierarchy of authority.

In the worldview of Neo-Marxist critical theory, authority is conferred not by wisdom, age, position, or experience but by victim status. Claims of oppression and victimization based on a subjective "lived experience" must be believed without question. Victim groups include non-whites, females, and so-called "sexual minorities" or members of the LGBTQIA+ community. The more victim boxes one can check, the greater their moral authority. The greater the authority, the greater the power. The granting of power and authority to victim groups naturally (and perversely) results in an explosion in the demand for victim status. Would-be victims are constantly on the lookout for opportunities to claim offense or harm, searching out ever smaller "microaggressions" to claim victimization.

Discussion Questions

- How does the redefinition of authority differ from the true definition? Discuss all that has changed.
- In what ways have you seen or experienced the redefinition of authority?
- What are some of the social and cultural changes that the redefinition of authority has brought about? What kinds of changes have resulted in policies and laws?

Personal Reflection and Application

Next week at home, take time to reflect on these areas of application. Read the questions and write down your responses.

The most basic level of authority is self-government, or what the Bible calls "self-control." Self-control is a "fruit" of the Holy Spirit (Galatians 5:22–23). We covered the vital importance of self-government in the freedom session.

Your roles of authority

Beyond self-government, write down your current roles of authority, such as a husband in marriage, a parent in the home, a supervisor at work, or even a coach on a sports team.

QUESTION: What is your attitude toward your role of authority? Do you see it as a burden, or do you even deny the role? How can you change your thinking about authority and see it as a God-given responsibility and opportunity to which you are accountable? What can you do to embrace that responsibility for the good of those under your leadership?

QUESTION: For each of your current roles of authority, what is one specific way you can lovingly and sacrificially serve those under your authority for their good, helping them grow, mature, and become all that God wants them to be?

Your roles in submission

Now write down the specific areas in which you are under someone else's authority. At the most basic level we are all under the supreme authority of God and his Word in Scripture, but what other God-given authorities are you currently in submission to?

QUESTION: Are you fully submitted to God, seeking his Kingdom and his righteousness first and seeking to do his will above all? Are you fully submitted to the authority of God's Word in Scripture, allowing it to guide all you do in every area of your life?

QUESTION: What is your attitude toward human authorities in your life? Are you resentful and begrudging toward authority, or do you gladly submit to the rightful authority of others, delighting to follow their lead and obey their commands?

Respectful disobedience

Legitimate human authorities must exercise their authority in ways that align with God's higher law in the Ten Commandments. In cases where human authorities compel those under their authority to violate God's higher law, those under their authority have a duty to respectfully disobey and be willing to face the consequences of their disobedience.

QUESTION: Are there any areas where this is the case in your life? What steps can you take to obey God's law, even if it means disobeying human authority?

Concluding Thoughts

Jesus Christ came to bring light, truth, and beauty into a world of darkness, lies, and despair. He came to bring his kingdom with its "right-side-up" value system, including true authority and hierarchy. After showing us what this looks like in practice, he commissioned his church to continue living out true authority.

Over the centuries many millions of Christians have faithfully, though imperfectly, followed the Lord's example. True authority has shaped entire cultures and nations. Its power to shape cultures in positive ways is immense.

RECOMMENDED RESOURCES

- *Servanthood: The Calling of Every Christian* by Darrow L. Miller (2009)
- *Lead Like Jesus: Lessons from the Greatest Leadership Role Model of All Time* by Ken Blanchard (2008)
- *Sphere Sovereignty: Church, State, Family, Education, and Business* by Abraham Kuyper, Translated into English by George Kamp (2024)

JUSTICE

Today, one of the most pervasive phrases in our culture is "social justice." It's everywhere in our education systems, business, sports, the media, and even in many of our churches. We are all encouraged to join in the fight for social justice.

But what exactly is social justice? How do its advocates define it? And is that definition different from the way the Bible defines justice?

Because justice is such a central word in the Bible, getting these questions right is critically important.

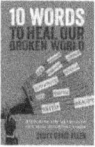

This week we're reading Chapter 7, "Justice," in *10 Words to Heal Our Broken World* by Scott David Allen.

PERSONAL BIBLE STUDY: *JUSTICE*

Before You Begin

In the space below write a concise, dictionary-style definition of justice from your current understanding without consulting sources such as a dictionary, the internet, or another person. The purpose is to record your current understanding and see how it changes due to this study.

BIBLE STUDY

Justice is conformity to a standard for moral goodness or righteousness. With that in mind, read the following passages and prayerfully respond to the question below.

> The LORD reigns, let the earth be glad; let the distant shores rejoice. Clouds and thick darkness surround him; righteousness and justice are the foundation of his throne. (Psalm 97:1–2)

> He is the Rock, his works are perfect, and all his ways are just. A faithful God who does no wrong, upright and just is he. (Deuteronomy 32:4)

> The LORD is righteous in all his ways. (Psalm 145:17)

> God is light; in him there is no darkness at all. (1 John 1:5)

QUESTION: According to these passages, what is the ultimate standard by which we determine what is just or unjust?

Reflect on these quotes from the *10 Words* book:

In the Bible, the Hebrew words tsedek *and* mishpat *are translated into English as "righteousness" or "justice," depending on the context. The Bible contains more than thirty examples of "righteousness" and "justice" being used interchangeably. Righteousness is synonymous with justice. Antonyms of justice are* injustice *or* evil.

Like a plumb line, justice is a standard or basis for righteousness. Justice is alignment to that standard. Where do we find this standard?

We find it in God, the Creator of the universe, whose very nature is goodness, righteousness, and holiness (or moral perfection). He is the moral plumb line determining what is good and right for all peoples and eras. And because God doesn't change, this standard doesn't change.

Read the following passages and prayerfully respond to the question below.

When the LORD finished speaking to Moses on Mount Sinai, he gave him the two tablets of the covenant law, the tablets of stone inscribed by the finger of God. (Exodus 31:18)

The law is holy, and the commandment is holy, righteous and good. (Romans 7:12)

When Gentiles, who do not have the law [the Ten Commandments], do by nature things required by the law . . . they show that the requirements of the law are written on their hearts, their consciences also bearing witness, and their thoughts sometimes accusing them and at other times even defending them. (Romans 2:14–15)

QUESTION: According to these passages, what are two ways God communicates his perfect moral standard for justice to all people?

Reflect on these quotes from the *10 Words* book:

A moral standard is commonly referred to as a law, which is why justice is equated with lawfulness and injustice with lawbreaking or lawlessness.

As John Calvin said, the law given to Moses reveals God's character. This law is one of God's greatest gifts because it provides the only sure and unchanging standard for justice in human history. This is why an image of Moses holding the two stone tablets is inscribed at the apex of the Supreme Court building in Washington, DC.

According to the great medieval theologian Thomas Aquinas, an unjust law is a human law that is not rooted in the eternal "law of God."

"There are two types of laws: just laws and unjust laws. I agree with Saint Augustine that an unjust law is no law. How do you determine when a law is just or unjust? A just law is a man-made code that squares with the moral law or the law of God. An unjust law is a code that is out of harmony with the moral law."—Martin Luther King Jr.[1]

Read the following passages and prayerfully respond to the question below.

He has shown you, O mortal, what is good. And what does the LORD require of you? To act justly and to love mercy and to walk humbly with your God. (Micah 6:8)

Put to death . . . sexual immorality, impurity, lust, evil desires and greed, which is idolatry. Because of these, the wrath of God is coming . . . But now you must also rid yourselves of all such things as these: anger, rage, malice, slander, and filthy language from your lips. Do not lie to each other . . . As God's chosen people, holy and dearly loved, clothe yourselves with compassion, kindness, humility, gentleness, and patience. Bear with each other and forgive one another if any of you has a grievance against someone. Forgive as the Lord forgave you. And over all these virtues put on love, which binds them all together in perfect unity. (Colossians 3:5–6, 12–14)

Each of you must put off falsehood and speak truthfully to your neighbor . . . Anyone who has been stealing must steal no longer but must work, doing something useful with their own hands, that they may have something to share with those in need. Do not let any unwholesome talk come out of your mouths, but only what is helpful for building others up . . . Get rid of all bitterness, rage and anger, brawling and slander, along with every form of malice. Be kind and compassionate to one another, forgiving each other, just as in Christ God forgave you. (Ephesians 4:25, 28–32)

QUESTION: What do these passages reveal about justice in our everyday lives? What does it mean to live justly?

Reflect on these quotes from the *10 Words* book:

What does justice look like in daily life? It means loving your neighbor as yourself, doing to others as you would have them do to you, and living in right relationships with God and others.

"We do justice when we give all human beings their due as creations of God."—Tim Keller.[2]

Justice requires recognizing what it means to be human—that all people possess inherent dignity and worth, with (in the Declaration's immortal phrasing) "unalienable rights" to life and liberty. To "do justice" is to treat others as uniquely valuable and to respect their God-given rights. It is the duty of every human being.

Read the following passages and prayerfully respond to the question below.

> Learn to do right; seek justice. Defend the oppressed. Take up the cause of the fatherless; plead the case of the widow. (Isaiah 1:17)

> If anyone is poor among your fellow Israelites in any of the towns of the land the LORD your God is giving you, do not be hardhearted or tightfisted toward them. Rather, be openhanded and freely lend them whatever they need. (Deuteronomy 15:7–8)

> "Is not this the kind of fasting [or worship] I have chosen: to loose the chains of injustice and untie the cords of the yoke, to set the oppressed free and break every yoke? Is it not to share your food with the hungry and provide the poor wanderer with shelter—when you see the naked, to clothe them, and not to turn away from your own flesh and blood?" (Isaiah 58:6–7)

QUESTION: What do these passages further reveal about what it means to act justly? To whom are we supposed to pay particular attention?

Reflect on these quotes from the *10 Words* book:

In our fallen world there will always be vulnerable, marginalized, and oppressed victims of injustice. Wars, disease, disasters, and human evil ensure that. Justice demands that we give special attention to these people. They, too, bear God's image and should be shown respect, treated with dignity, defended, protected, and tenderly cared for.

But how we do this matters greatly and requires careful discernment. If people are poor because they refuse to work or prefer to live lives of dependency on the generosity of others, they need to be encouraged to work and provide for themselves and others. Giving able-bodied people handouts does harm to their human dignity by treating them like animals. See 2 Thessalonians 6:10, Ephesians 4:28, and 1 Timothy 5:3–16.

Read the following passages and prayerfully respond to the question below.

God will bring every deed into judgment, including every hidden thing, whether it is good or evil. (Ecclesiastes 12:14)

The LORD reigns forever; he has established his throne for judgment. He rules the world in righteousness and judges the peoples with equity. (Psalm 9:7–8)

[God] has set a day when he will judge the world with justice by the man he has appointed. He has given proof of this to everyone by raising him from the dead. (Acts 17:31)

We must all appear before the judgment seat of Christ so that each of us may receive what is due us for the things done while in the body, whether good or bad. (2 Corinthians 5:10)

QUESTION: As we've seen, justice involves living justly or doing what is morally good in our daily lives, particularly regarding the poor and vulnerable. According to the passages above, what else does justice involve?

Reflect on these quotes from the *10 Words* book:

Justice requires that evil and injustice be judged and punished because if evil goes unpunished, injustice multiplies. Justice means exacting an appropriate payment for a crime. No payment, no justice. We commonly say that lawbreakers must be held "to account" for their crimes, bringing to mind accounting concepts such as debts, payments, and balance sheets. Proper accounting requires that the books be balanced. So does justice.

The popular image of justice is of a blindfolded woman with balanced scales in one hand and a sword in the other. The blindfold represents the impartiality before the law that a just decision requires. The scales represent the balance that justice demands. The sword represents the punishment due to lawbreakers. Those who commit injustice incur a debt against their victims, and the scale is out of balance. That debt may be stolen property, freedom, innocence, reputation, or even life. Justice demands that balance be restored—the debt has to be paid.

When Christ returns, he will establish his throne of judgment. Every act of human evil and injustice will be accounted for, judged, and punished, for, in the end, perfect righteousness will prevail.

Read the following passages and prayerfully respond to the questions below.

[Parents,] do not withhold discipline from a child; if you punish them with the rod, they will not die. Punish them with the rod and save them from death. (Proverbs 23:13–14)

"If your brother or sister sins, go and point out their fault, just between the two of you. If they listen to you, you have won them over. But if they will not listen, take one or two others along so that 'every matter may be established by the testimony of two or three witnesses.' If they still refuse to listen, tell it to the church [elders], and if they refuse to listen even to the church, treat them as you would a pagan or a tax collector." (Matthew 18:15–17)

Rulers (civil authorities) hold no terror for those who do right, but for those who do wrong. Do you want to be free from fear of the one in authority? Then do what is right and you will be commended. For the one in authority is God's servant for your good. But if you do wrong, be afraid, for rulers do not bear the sword for no reason. They are God's servants, agents of wrath to bring punishment on the wrongdoer.

QUESTION: God is the supreme judge, but he has delegated responsibility for upholding justice to certain human authorities. Based on the passages above, who are those human authorities?

QUESTION: Over whom do they have the responsibility to judge and punish wrongdoing?

QUESTION: What happens if they fail to carry out this responsibility?

Reflect on this quote from the *10 Words* book:

Justice that involves rendering judgment and punishing wrongdoing is reserved for God-ordained authorities, including parents in the home, elders in the church, and civil authorities in the state. This aspect of justice demands that authorities render judgments fairly, punish injustice, and treat everyone equally before the law because that is how God—the supreme authority in the universe—treats us.

Read the following passages and prayerfully respond to the questions below.

The LORD your God . . . shows no partiality and accepts no bribes. (Deuteronomy 10:17)

You shall do no injustice in court. You shall not be partial to the poor or defer to the great, but in righteousness shall you judge your neighbor. (Leviticus 19:15 ESV)

One witness is not enough to convict anyone accused of any crime or offense they may have committed. A matter must be established by the testimony of two or three witnesses. (Deuteronomy 19:15. See also 2 Corinthians 13:1)

You shall not give false testimony against your neighbor. (Exodus 20:16)

My brothers and sisters . . . [you] must not show favoritism. Suppose a man comes into your meeting wearing a gold ring and fine clothes, and a poor man in filthy old clothes also comes in. If you show special attention to the man wearing fine clothes and say, "Here's a good seat for you," but say to the poor man . . . "Sit on the floor by my feet," have you not discriminated among yourselves and become judges with evil thoughts? (James 2:1–4)

Brothers and sisters, if someone is caught in a sin, you who live by the Spirit should restore that person gently. (Galatians 6:1)

The punishment inflicted on [the wrongdoer] by the majority is sufficient. Now . . . you ought to forgive and comfort him, so that he will not be overwhelmed by excessive sorrow. (2 Corinthians 2:6–7)

QUESTION: What principles of justice do the passages above reveal about *how* human authorities should judge and punish injustice?

QUESTION: How did these principles shape our justice systems in Western culture, giving rise to concepts such as "due process?"

Reflect on this quote from the *10 Words* book:
True justice demands that authorities render judgments in a fair, unbiased, and impartial way based on the testimony of two or three witnesses. Punishment must not be excessive and must be aimed at restoration. Witnesses must speak truthfully. Earthly judges must treat everyone equally before the law because that is how God—the supreme authority in the universe—treats us. He impartially rewards good and punishes evil. He does not ignore the sins of any. He does not take bribes.

Read the following passages and prayerfully respond to the question below.

The LORD saw that the wickedness of man was great in the earth, and that every intention of the thoughts of his heart was only evil continually. (Genesis 6:5 ESV)

The heart [of man] is deceitful above all things, and desperately wicked. (Jeremiah 17:9 KJV)

"For . . . out of the heart of man, come evil thoughts, sexual immorality, theft, murder, adultery, coveting, wickedness, deceit, sensuality, envy, slander, pride, foolishness. All these evil things come from within and defile a person." (Mark 7:21–23 ESV)

All have sinned and fall short of the glory of God. (Romans 3:23)

As it is written: "None is righteous, no, not one; no one understands; no one seeks for God. All have turned aside; together they have become worthless; no one does good, not even one." (Romans 3:10–12 ESV)

QUESTION: Based on these passages, who is guilty before God of injustice?

Reflect on these quotes from the *10 Words* book:
Take a look at the Ten Commandments in Exodus 20:1–17. How do you measure up? If we're honest, we'll admit that we all fall short against the only standard that ultimately matters.

"The line separating good and evil passes not through states, nor between classes, nor between political parties either—but right through every human heart"—Aleksandr Solzhenitsyn[3]

Read the following passages and prayerfully respond to the questions below.

Your throne, O God, will last for ever and ever; a scepter of justice will be the scepter of your kingdom; You love righteousness and hate wickedness. (Psalm 45:6–7)

[God] will deliver the needy who cry out, the afflicted who have no one to help. He will take pity on the weak and the needy and save the needy from death. He will rescue them from oppression and violence, for precious is their blood in his sight. (Psalm 72:12–14)

The wrath of God is being revealed from heaven against all the godlessness and wickedness of people, who suppress the truth by their wickedness. (Romans 1:18)

Because of your stubbornness and your unrepentant heart, you are storing up wrath against yourself for the day of God's wrath, when his righteous judgment will be revealed. (Romans 2:5)

"It is mine to avenge; I will repay," says the Lord. (Romans 12:19)

I saw heaven standing open and there before me was a white horse, whose rider is called Faithful and True. With justice he judges . . . His eyes are like blazing fire, and on his head are many crowns . . . Coming out of his mouth is a sharp sword with which to strike down the nations. "He will rule them with an iron scepter." He treads the winepress of the fury of the wrath of God Almighty. On his robe and on his thigh he has this name written: KING OF KINGS AND LORD OF LORDS. (Revelation 19:11–13; 15–16)

QUESTION: What is God's reaction to the evil and injustice in the world? How will he respond to it?

QUESTION: How does Psalm 72:14 reveal God's heart for the victims of injustice and oppression?

Reflect on these quotes from the *10 Words* book:

God isn't indifferent to injustice. It is abhorrent and intolerable to him. Today Christians are uncomfortable talking about God's wrath. We prefer to dwell on his love, mercy, and forgiveness. Those are all wonderfully true, but our picture of him is incomplete if we fail to reckon with God's hatred of injustice.

God's compassion stirs in him a hatred for injustice. He rises in anger against those who oppress the weak, the marginalized, and the poor. He will hold every oppressor accountable.

This is bad news for all of us because we are all lawbreakers. We are all guilty of evil and injustice to one degree or another. We are all objects of God's wrath and fully deserve punishment for our wrongdoings.

Read the following passage and prayerfully respond to the questions below.

> Then the LORD came down in the cloud and stood there with [Moses] and proclaimed his name, the LORD. And he passed in front of Moses, proclaiming, "The LORD, the LORD, the compassionate and gracious God, slow to anger, abounding in love and faithfulness, maintaining love to thousands, and forgiving wickedness, rebellion and sin. Yet he does not leave the guilty unpunished; he punishes the children and their children for the sin of the parents to the third and fourth generation." (Exodus 34:5–7)

This famous passage records the longest name of God in the Bible. His names reveal the essence of his character. Write down each word or phrase in these verses that describes God's character.

QUESTION: How are God's mercy and justice revealed in this name?

QUESTION: Mercy is forgiveness shown toward someone by a person with the authority to judge and punish them. If God hates evil, and justice demands that every act of human lawlessness and evil be judged and punished, how can God be *both* just and merciful?

Read the following passages and prayerfully respond to the questions below.

"God so loved the world that he gave his one and only Son, that whoever believes in him shall not perish but have eternal life." (John 3:16)

At just the right time, when we were still powerless, Christ died for the ungodly . . . God demonstrates his own love for us in this: While we were still sinners, Christ died for us. Since we have now been justified by his blood, how much more shall we be saved from God's wrath through him! (Romans 5:6, 8–9)

Surely, he took up our pain and bore our suffering, yet we considered him punished by God, stricken by him, and afflicted. But he was pierced for our transgressions; he was crushed for our iniquities; the punishment that brought us peace was on him, and by his wounds we are healed. We all, like sheep, have gone astray; each of us has turned to our own way, and the LORD has laid on him the iniquity of us all. (Isaiah 53:4–6)

If we confess our sins, he is faithful and just and will forgive us our sins and purify us from all unrighteousness. (1 John 1:9)

QUESTION: How does the cross of Jesus Christ display God's justice and mercy?

QUESTION: According to 1 John 1:9, how do we receive God's forgiveness for our sins?

QUESTION: Reflect on the importance of justice and mercy. What would society look like if there was justice but no mercy? What would it look like if there was mercy but no justice?

Reflect on these quotes from the *10 Words* book:

God's goodness expresses itself in both justice and mercy. If mercy means overlooking injustice, this presents a seeming dilemma. How can God be merciful and yet uphold justice? We find the answer at the apex of God's extraordinary story of redemption—the life, death, and resurrection of Jesus Christ. In an act of sheer love, God incarnate took upon himself the punishment we deserved for our transgressions to uphold the righteous demand of justice and show us a mercy we could never deserve. Through the cross of Jesus Christ, God provides a way of escaping the punishment and wrath that our rebellion has earned us—a way that displays God's glory in all its radiant splendor.

God delays the final judgment for the moment, knowing full well that evil and injustice will continue in this fallen world. He delays his ultimate judgment, not because he is powerless over evil or lacks compassion for its victims. He delays it for the sake of mercy, for God is "patient . . . not wanting anyone to perish, but everyone to come to repentance" (2 Peter 3:9). But his patience won't last forever. When Jesus returns, he will be Judge, and perfect justice will be done.

In Revelation 20:11–15 we read about the final judgment, where we will all stand before Christ's judgment seat and books will be opened. One will contain a record of everything we've ever done. Every one of our thoughts and actions will be judged against God's perfect moral standard. Nothing will be hidden. There will be no escaping justice. But mercifully, there is another book—the Book of Life. It, too, contains a record. It lists the names of those who, though guilty, have received mercy simply by requesting it. How? The punishment for their lawbreaking was paid for on the cross. In the final judgment it won't matter if you are male or female, black or white, rich or poor. The only divide that will matter will be between the "poor in spirit" who cry out for mercy and the proud who do not.

LEARNING TOGETHER: *JUSTICE*

Welcome and Opening Prayer

Opening Discussion

Discuss together what you learned about justice during your personal study. What ideas stood out to you? How did God speak to you through the Scriptures?

Watch the Video and Discuss the Questions Below
Note: You'll find the "justice" video at 10WordsBook.org.

- What insights did you gain from the video about justice?
- What insights did you gain about the redefinition of justice?

Definitions and Discussion

Read the two definitions and quotes below. Discuss the contemporary redefinition of authority and its cultural consequences.

JUSTICE

Conformity to God's moral standard as revealed in the Ten Commandments and the Royal Law: "love your neighbor as yourself." Communitive justice: living in right relationship with God and others; giving people their due as image-bearers of God. Distributive justice: impartially rendering judgment, righting wrongs, and meting out punishment for lawbreaking. Reserved for God and God-ordained authorities including parents in the home, elders in the church, teachers in the school, and civil authorities in the state.[1]

JUSTICE REDEFINED

Deconstructing traditional systems and structures deemed to be oppressive, and redistributing power and resources from oppressors to their victims in the pursuit of equality of outcome.

Reflect on these quotes from the *10 Words* book:

Today, an ideology (and accompanying movement) described by its adherents as "social justice" has radically redefined the biblical understanding of justice. This new ideology is characterized by its obsession with power, oppression, and victimization; its use of tactics reminiscent of Mao's Cultural Revolution and an "end justifies the means" methodology; and its fixation on class, race, gender, and sexual orientation as defining characteristics of personal identity; this is deeply hostile toward Judeo-Christian religion, particularly in its beliefs about family and sexuality. It is obsessed with "equity," or the redistribution of wealth and power from oppressors to victims by an ever-larger state.

"For many, especially the young, discovering a new meaning [for life] . . . is thrilling. Social justice ideology does everything a religion should. It offers an account of the whole: that human life and society . . . must be seen entirely as a function of social power structures, in

which various groups have spent all human existence oppressing other groups, and it provides a set of principles to resist and reverse this interlocking web of oppression."—Andrew Sullivan[4]

According to the social justice narrative, what is our fundamental problem as human beings? It is "oppression" by white, heteronormative males who have established and maintain hegemonic power structures to oppress and subjugate women, people of color, sexual minorities (LGBTQ+), and others. What's the solution? Revolution! Victims and their allies must unite to unmask, deconstruct, and overthrow these oppressive power structures, systems, and institutions.

In the zero-sum world of social justice power struggles, there is no "live and let live" tolerance, win-win, or compromise. There is no place for forgiveness or grace, no "love your enemy," no "first get the log out of your own eye" introspection. There is only grievance, condemnation, and retribution. Bigots, haters, and oppressors must be destroyed.

Over the past decade we've experienced nothing short of a moral revolution. Things that were formerly understood to be good—such as hard work; punctuality; freedom of speech; freedom of religion; reserving sex until marriage; marriage as the exclusive, lifelong union of a man and a woman; and even the male-female binary itself—are increasingly understood to be bigoted, hateful, and discriminatory— tools of oppression.

According to social justice ideology, people are not free, responsible moral agents but victims or beneficiaries of oppressive systems. Moral guilt or innocence is not a function of individual choices but of group identity. If you are a victim, you are morally innocent. If you are an oppressor, you are morally guilty regardless of your actions, and no justification is possible.

The false system of moral guilt and innocence at the heart of social justice morality makes it incompatible with the gospel. It is a false gospel. It promises justification, not by grace alone through faith in Christ but by membership in a victim group.

The word equity has an almost sacred connotation in the worldview of ideological social justice. Equality is a profoundly biblical idea. In the Bible, this parity refers to the equality that all human beings possess as image-bearers of God. In the classical Marxist worldview, however, equity means equality of outcome—in other words, sameness, uniformity, and interchangeability. Ironically, despite its proclaimed commitment to "diversity," the actual outworking of ideological social justice is to make diverse people the same.

What do we lose if ideological social justice continues to eclipse biblical justice? We are already seeing change and should expect much more: Less gratitude and more grievance. Less personal responsibility and more claims of victimhood, hostility, division, and blame casting. Continued erosion of the rule of law, with moral norms and laws becoming arbitrary, constantly changing, conforming to the whims of whatever group can marshal power to sway popular opinion. The loss of due process; no more "innocent until proven guilty." The loss of free speech and the ability to openly debate and discuss challenging topics. The loss of any basis for civility, social unity, cohesion, or tolerance.

Discussion Questions

- How does the redefinition of justice differ from the true definition? Discuss all that has changed.
- In what ways have you seen or experienced the redefinition of justice?
- What are some of the social and cultural changes that the redefinition of justice has brought about? What kinds of changes have resulted in policies and laws?

Personal Reflection and Application

Next week at home, reflect on these application questions and write down your responses.

As followers of Jesus Christ, we must reject the false presuppositions of social justice and unapologetically embrace and advocate for true, biblical justice in the home, the church, and every sphere of society where we have influence.

QUESTION: Based on what you have learned in this session, what changes do you need to make in your thinking about justice?

Justice involves living justly or doing what is morally good in our daily lives. We don't do this to earn God's favor or merit our salvation. Christ has already accomplished this on our behalf. But we are saved and justified to live holy, just lives. Review the Ten Commandments in Exodus 20:1–17 and the detailed descriptions of what justice means in our daily lives found in Ephesians 4:25–32 and Colossians 3:5–14.

QUESTION: In what areas are you falling short of God's moral standard in your own life? Be as specific as possible. Confess your shortcomings to God, pray for his help and strength to live in obedience, and make a plan to change.

Living justly also involves paying particular attention to victims of injustice, including the poor and vulnerable in our families, churches, and communities, and tenderly caring for their needs.

QUESTION: Who are these people in our life? Because they are on the margins of society, they are often easy to overlook, so think carefully as you answer.

QUESTION: What one thing can you do to defend victims of injustice and care for the poor, weak, and vulnerable around you?

Justice requires that evil and injustice be judged and punished because if evil goes unpunished, injustice multiplies. God is the supreme judge, but he has delegated responsibility for upholding justice by rendering judgment and punishment for wrongdoing to parents in the home, elders in the church, and civil authorities in the government.

QUESTION: What roles of authority has God currently delegated to you to judge and punish wrongdoing?

Most people have this responsibility as parents, but we live at a time when there is significant social pressure to abdicate or neglect discipling our children. Yet the Bible speaks very clearly about this vital area of responsibility. Review these passages and answer the questions below: Proverbs 13:24; 19:18; 22:6; 22:15; 23:13–14; 29:15; and Ephesians 6:4.

QUESTION: In what way do you need to think and act differently about your responsibility to uphold justice in the home by carefully and consistently disciplining your children?

If you are a church elder, a civil magistrate, or a teacher, you may also be subject to social pressure to abdicate or neglect your responsibilities to judge and punish wrongdoing.

QUESTION: If you are in one of these roles, how do you need to think and act differently about your responsibility to uphold justice?

For those responsible for rendering judgment and punishing wrongdoing, the Bible provides many principles for how this ought to be done. Review these passages and answer the question below: Exodus 20:16; Leviticus 19:15; Deuteronomy 10:17; 19:5; 2 Corinthians 2:6–7; 13:1; Galatians 6:1; James 2:1–4.

QUESTION: Based on these principles, what changes do you need to make to the way you render judgment and punish wrongdoing?

The ideology of social justice, with roots in Marxist worldview assumptions, is now dominant in Western institutions of education, business, government, entertainment, media, and the legal profession. It is now shaping how many Christian pastors understand and teach about justice in the church.

QUESTION: How can you oppose this dangerous cultural counterfeit and defend true justice in your sphere of influence?

Concluding Thoughts

"Biblical Christianity and ideological social justice are distinct and incompatible worldviews. They are opposed in their understanding of reality, power, authority, human nature, morality, epistemology, and much more. These differences matter. They will inevitably lead to vastly different kinds of societies. The culture that is emerging around us from the worldview of critical social theory is one marked by hostility, division, and a false sense of moral superiority. It is a culture where truth is replaced by power and gratitude by grievance. A culture in which your identity is defined by your tribe and your tribe is always in conflict with other tribes.

The hour is late, but I believe there is still time. We, the Bible-believing church, must humble ourselves, cry out to God, and courageously defend the truth against the greatest worldview threat of our generation."[5]

RECOMMENDED RESOURCES

Books

- *Why Social Justice is Not Biblical Justice: An Urgent Appeal to Fellow Christians in a Time of Social Crisis* by Scott D. Allen (2020)
- *Confronting Injustice without Compromising Truth: 12 Questions Christians Should Ask About Social Justice* by Thaddeus J. Williams (2020)
- *Christianity and Wokeness: How the Social Justice Movement Is Hijacking the Gospel and the Way to Stop It* by Owen Strachan (2021)
- *America's Cultural Revolution: How the Radical Left Conquered Everything* by Christopher F. Rufo (2023)

Video

- The Bible Project: *Justice • This Is the Bible's Radical View, youtube. com/watch?v=A14THPoc4-4*

FAITH

What is faith?

The Merriam-Webster dictionary defines faith as a "firm belief in something for which there is no proof."[1] It is a "blind leap" into the unknown.

Others think of faith as the power of belief. If you truly believe with all your heart, is the supposition, you can make your dreams come true.

Faith is one of the most important words in the Bible, so Christians must understand it accurately.

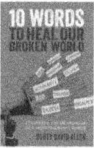

This week we're reading Chapter 8, "Faith," in 10 Words to Heal Our Broken World by Scott David Allen.

PERSONAL BIBLE STUDY: *FAITH*

Before You Begin

In the space below write a concise, dictionary-style definition of faith from your current understanding without consulting sources such as a dictionary, the internet, or another person. The purpose is to record your current understanding and see how it changes due to this study.

BIBLE STUDY

Read the following passages and prayerfully respond to the question below.

The Berean Jews were of more noble character than those in Thessalonica, for they received the message with great eagerness and examined the Scriptures every day to see if what Paul said was true. (Acts 17:11)

If Christ has not been raised [from the dead], our preaching is useless and so is your faith. More than that, we are then found to be false witnesses about God . . . If Christ has not been raised, your faith is futile; you are still in your sins. (1 Corinthians 15:14–17)

Always be prepared to give an answer to everyone who asks you to give the reason for the hope that you have. But do this with gentleness and respect. (1 Peter 3:15)

QUESTION: What is the relationship between faith and truth, according to these passages?

Reflect on these quotes from the *10 Words* book:

Faith is synonymous with trust and trustworthiness. Words that express the opposite of faith include distrust, doubt, anxiety, fear, insecurity, skepticism, unsureness, *and* indecision.

The Old Testament Hebrew word for faith is emet, *the same as the Hebrew word for truth. Emet refers to faithfulness, reliability, trustworthiness, and dependability. It relates to something real and entirely truthful. The New Testament Greek word for faith is* pistis, *connoting evidence and moral conviction. It comes from* pietho, *which means convincing by argument and assenting to the evidence.*

Christian faith isn't believing in a beautiful myth or fairy tale because we want it to be true. It isn't a "blind leap" without regard to the evidence—just the opposite. Christian faith is taking actions based on the weight of the evidence—based on what is historically true.

Faith means trusting someone or something based on the weight of evidence. It means trusting in the truthfulness and reliability of something or someone based on personal experience and carefully researching available evidence.

To exercise faith, you begin with questions like these: Is that person trustworthy and dependable? Did that event actually happen? Is that thing safe or reliable? Can I trust it? You then seek answers to such questions by honestly searching for the truth. You observe carefully. You gather evidence. You listen carefully and analyze the evidence by applying reason and logic. This is exactly what the New Testament (Greek) word for faith (pistis) means.

We tend to think about faith in terms of "religion," but faith is not exclusive to religious people. It is a basic necessity of life for everyone. We exercise faith in hundreds of ways daily, often without realizing it. Without faith, getting out of bed each morning would be virtually impossible.

Genuine faith always has an object. It is faith in something or someone. "We all trust [or have faith] in something. Even the most skeptical among us exercises complete trust in many things. When we stand up, we trust that our legs will hold us. When we sit down, we trust the chair. We trust that, when we inhale, the right amount of oxygen will be present to sustain us. When we go to bed, we trust that the earth will continue its rotation so that morning will come. We have chosen to place trust in these things because of their past reliability. We choose to trust; otherwise, we would live in a constant state of fear and uncertainty."[2]

Read the following passage and prayerfully respond to the question below.

> What good is it, my brothers and sisters, if someone claims to have faith but has no deeds? Can such faith save them? Suppose a brother or a sister is without clothes and daily food. If one of you says to them, "Go in peace; keep warm and well fed," but does nothing about their physical needs, what good is it? In the same way, faith by itself, if it is not accompanied by action, is dead. But someone will say, "You have faith; I have deeds." Show me your faith without deeds, and I will show you my faith by my deeds." (James 2:14–18)

QUESTION: For faith to be genuine, what must it lead to (or result in)?

Reflect on these quotes from the *10 Words* book:

Faith involves the all-important concept of "assent." To exercise faith, you gather evidence for the truthfulness or trustworthiness of something or someone. Then you begin to form tentative conclusions. And then, in an all-important final step, you assent to the evidence by taking action based on those conclusions. This final step in the process is the essence of faith.

Your actions prove your faith. In other words, I can tell what you truly trust by your behavior.

Here's an everyday example of faith. You plan to visit a family member in another state by traveling on a commercial airliner. You've never flown before, so you have a question: Is flying in a commercial airliner safe? You then seek to answer the question by carefully observing and gathering evidence. You might look at the safety track record of airline travel. You might talk to people you trust who travel frequently, and you might question pilots or others who fly for a living.

Then, after careful, logical thought and reasoning, you conclude that airline travel appears safe. You've convinced yourself intellectually. But for that belief to become faith, you must assent to the evidence by purchasing a ticket and getting on an airplane. The essence of genuine faith is this final step: getting on the aircraft and flying. Once you do this, you add your personal experience to the evidence. Your faith grows stronger the more personal experience you have. Your trust in the reliability and dependability of airline travel grows as you exercise faith with each subsequent trip.

Christian faith involves complete surrender, which involves a changed way of living that will show itself in our actions. Will we trust Jesus with our income? With our career? With our life? With our family? Our behavior will reveal to the watching world whether our faith is genuine.

Read the following passages and prayerfully respond to the questions below.

The wrath of God is being revealed from heaven against all the godlessness and wickedness of people, who suppress the truth by their wickedness, since what may be known about God is plain to them because God has made it plain to them. For since the creation of the world God's invisible qualities— his eternal power and divine nature—have been clearly seen, being understood from what has been made, so that people are without excuse. (Romans 1:18–20)

In the past God spoke to our ancestors through the prophets at many times and in various ways, but in these last days he has spoken to us by his Son, whom he appointed heir of all things, and through whom also he made the universe. (Hebrews 1:1–2)

QUESTION: Based on these passages, Christian faith is a firm belief in what?

QUESTION: In Romans 1:18–21 Paul claims that God's existence is "clearly seen" by everyone. How?

QUESTION: Today, in our secular world, many influential people claim that the God of Genesis 1:1 does not exist. They also claim that their conclusion is factual and not based on "faith." Given Paul's assertion in Romans 1:18–20, how would you respond to them? See the footnote for more information.[3]

Reflect on this quote from the *10 Words* book:
Christian faith is grounded on a firm trust that God exists as the Creator of the universe and that he has communicated to us reliably through the Bible.

Read the following passages and prayerfully respond to the questions below.

[At the end of the apostle John's gospel, he wrote,] The man who saw it has given testimony, and his testimony is true. He knows that he tells the truth, and he testifies so that you also may believe. (John 19:35)

Many have undertaken to draw up an account of the things that have been fulfilled among us, just as they were handed down to us by those who, from the first, were eyewitnesses and servants of the word. With this in mind, since I [Luke, the author of The Gospel of Luke] have carefully investigated everything from the beginning, I too decided to write an orderly account for you, most excellent Theophilus, so that you may know the certainty of what you have been taught. (Luke 1:1–4)

That which was from the beginning, which we have heard, which we have seen with our eyes, which we have looked at and our hands have touched—this we proclaim concerning the Word of life. The life appeared; we have seen it and testify to it, and we proclaim to you . . . what we have seen and heard so that you also may have fellowship with us. And our fellowship is with the Father and with his Son, Jesus Christ. (1 John 1:1–3)

We did not follow cleverly devised myths when we made known to you the power and coming of our Lord Jesus Christ, but we were eyewitnesses of his majesty. (2 Peter 1:16 ESV)

QUESTION: These passages were all written by close followers of Jesus or those who knew them intimately. What claims are they making about their written accounts?

QUESTION: Why can we trust the truthfulness and historical reliability of the Bible? See footnote for more information.[4]

Reflect on this quote from the *10 Words* book:

There is nothing wrong with being skeptical and doubting at the beginning of a process of honest examination, particularly of claims as audacious as the gospel makes. Don't be afraid to ask the hardest questions you have. Seeking honest answers to questions is how Christian faith is built and strengthened.

But once you reach the point where you are convinced that the evidence points overwhelmingly to the truthfulness of the gospel, continuing to doubt is counterproductive. It often reflects a proud, rebellious heart. This is why James wrote that when you ask God for wisdom, "you must believe and not doubt, because the one who doubts is like a wave of the sea, blown and tossed by the wind. That person should not expect to receive anything from the Lord. Such a person is double-minded and unstable in all they do" (James 1:6–8).

**Read the following passages and prayerfully respond to the
questions below.**

As for you, you were dead in your transgressions and sins
. . . But because of his great love for us, God, who is rich in
mercy, made us alive with Christ even when we were dead in
transgressions—it is by grace you have been saved. And God
raised us up with Christ and seated us with him in the heavenly
realms in Christ Jesus, in order that in the coming ages he
might show the incomparable riches of his grace, expressed in
his kindness to us in Christ Jesus. For it is by grace you have
been saved, through faith—and this is not from yourselves,
it is the gift of God—not by works, so that no one can boast.
(Ephesians 2:1, 4–9)

But now the righteousness of God has been manifested apart
from the law, although the Law and the Prophets bear witness
to it—the righteousness of God through faith in Jesus Christ
for all who believe. For there is no distinction: for all have
sinned and fall short of the glory of God, and are justified by
his grace as a gift, through the redemption that is in Christ
Jesus, whom God put forward as a propitiation by his blood,
to be received by faith. (Romans 3:21–25 ESV)

A person is not justified by the works of the law, but by faith in
Jesus Christ. So we, too, have put our faith in Christ Jesus that
we may be justified by faith in Christ and not by the works of
the law, because by the works of the law no one will be justified.
(Galatians 2:16)

QUESTION: According to Ephesians 2, verse 1, what was our condition when separated from Jesus Christ?

QUESTION: Based on these passages, how are we saved from sin and death and made right ("justified") with God?

QUESTION: How are we *not* saved?

Reflect on these quotes from the *10 Words* book:

The ground of saving faith is the finished work of Christ on the cross. It begins with questions like these: "Is Jesus Christ who he claimed to be?" "Did he die on a Roman cross, exchanging his perfect righteousness for my sins and paying the penalty I deserved?" "Could this incredibly good news be true?" To seek honest answers and to conclude that "yes, these things are true" is to come right to the doorstep of salvation. But saving faith requires that you (with the indispensable help of the Holy Spirit) step through the door. That final step involves more than belief in historical facts; it involves complete trust in Jesus, expressed through total surrender to Jesus as King and Lord. Saving faith is not mere belief or intellectual assent but complete trust in, and total surrender to, the risen and living Christ, the Savior of the world and the King of heaven and earth.

We can't earn our salvation through "good works." Our sin runs too deep. We can only accept the free gift of salvation through faith marked by humble confession of our sins, repentance, submission, and obedience. This is saving faith. It is the faith of the famous Reformation cry "Sola Fide." By faith alone we are saved—faith in the finished work of Jesus Christ on the cross on our behalf.

Read the following passages and prayerfully respond to the questions below.

Faith is the assurance of things hoped for, the conviction of things not seen. (Hebrews 11:1 ESV)

The LORD had said to Abram, "Go from your country, your people, and your father's household to the land I will show you. I will make you into a great nation, and I will bless you; I will make your name great, and . . . all the peoples on earth will be blessed through you." (Genesis 12:1–3)

[God promised Abraham,] "I will make your descendants as numerous as the stars in the sky and give them all these lands, and through your offspring, all nations on earth will be blessed." (Genesis 26:4)

Without weakening in his faith, [Abraham] faced the fact that his body was as good as dead—since he was about a hundred years old—and that [his wife] Sarah's womb was also dead. Yet he did not waver through unbelief regarding the promise of God but was strengthened in his faith and gave glory to God, being fully persuaded that God had the power to do what he had promised. (Romans 4:19–21)

By faith . . . Sarah, who was past childbearing age, was enabled to bear children [her son, Isaac] because she considered [God] faithful who had made the promise. (Hebrews 11:11)

By faith, Abraham, when God tested him, offered Isaac as a sacrifice. He who had embraced the promises was about to sacrifice his one and only son, even though God had said to him, "It is through Isaac that your offspring will be reckoned." Abraham reasoned that God could even raise the dead, and so, in a manner of speaking, he did receive Isaac back from death. (Hebrews 11:17–19)

Every word of God is flawless. (Proverbs 30:5)

No matter how many promises God has made, they are "Yes" in Christ. (2 Corinthians 1:20)

[Christ's] divine power has given us everything we need for a godly life through our knowledge of him, who called us by his own glory and goodness. Through these, he has given us his very great and precious promises so that through them you may participate in the divine nature. (2 Peter 1:3–4)

QUESTION: Hebrews 11:1 is one of the most important biblical passages on faith. How does the story of Abraham, Sarah, and Isaac help us understand the meaning of faith according to Hebrews 11:1? What is it that they did they "not see" yet still had complete trust (or assurance) in?

QUESTION: Like Abraham and Sarah, in what can we have complete assurance?

Reflect on these quotes from the *10 Words* book:

God is a promise-making, promise-keeping God. Like Abraham and Sarah, we, too, can have faith in God and his promises. He never lies, deceives, or changes like shifting sands. His word is rock-solid.

"Biblical faith is not a vague hope grounded in imaginary, wishful thinking. Instead, faith is a settled confidence that something in the future—something that is not yet seen but has been promised by God—will actually come to pass because God will bring it about."[5]

Read the following passages and prayerfully respond to the question below.

The LORD is trustworthy in all he promises and faithful in all he does. (Psalm 145:13)

The righteous person will live by his faithfulness. (Habakkuk 2:4; see also Romans 1:17, Galatians 3:11, and Hebrews 10:38)

Trust in the LORD with all your heart and lean not on your own understanding; in all your ways, submit to him, and he will make your paths straight. (Proverbs 3:5–6)

[A man brought his son to Jesus to be healed. He said,] "If you can do anything, take pity on us and help us."

"'If you can'?" said Jesus. "Everything is possible for one who believes." Immediately the boy's father exclaimed, "I do believe; help me overcome my unbelief!" (Mark 9:22–24)

Without faith, it is impossible to please God, because anyone who comes to him must believe that he exists and that he rewards those who earnestly seek him. (Hebrews 11:6)

QUESTION: What do we learn about faith from these passages?

Reflect on this quote from the *10 Words* book:
The righteous shall live by his faith (Habakkuk 2:4). By his faith in God. By trusting in God and his promises, not by trusting in himself or his own strength. Our faith in God is a lifelong process of growth, whereby over time, as we step out in faith, we experience God's faithfulness in our lives, and our faith grows stronger.

LEARNING TOGETHER: *FAITH*

Welcome and Opening Prayer

Opening Discussion
Discuss together what you learned about faith during your personal study. What ideas stood out to you? How did God speak to you through the Scriptures?

Watch the Video and Discuss the Questions Below
Note: You'll find the "faith" video at 10WordsBook.org.
- What insights did you gain from the video about faith?
- What insights did you gain about the redefinition of faith?

Definitions and Discussion
Read the two definitions and quotes below. Discuss the contemporary redefinition of faith and its cultural consequences.

FAITH

To assent to the weight of evidence; to trust in the truthfulness and reliability of something or someone based on a careful search of available evidence and personal experience.

FAITH REDEFINED

Affirming the truthfulness of something without regard to evidence, or even despite a lack of evidence.

Reflect on these quotes from the *10 Words* book:

Mark Twain once quipped, "Having faith is believing in something you just know ain't true." Tragically, this misconception about faith is now fully institutionalized in the West. The Oxford Dictionary of the English Language defines faith this way: "A strong belief in God or the doctrines of a religion, based on spiritual apprehension rather than proof."

In his book The Selfish Gene, *celebrity atheist Richard Dawkins states without fear of pushback that faith is "blind trust, in the absence of evidence, even in the teeth of evidence," while Bertrand Russell defines faith as "a firm belief in something for which there is no evidence."* [6]

According to people like Dawkins, Christianity is a clever fairy tale. If you want to believe in it despite the lack of evidence, that is your business, but you must keep that belief private. The public realm must be guided by facts and science, not religion. Today many people, sadly including many Christians, have entirely accepted this narrative. Under the influence of public figures such as Dawkins, they see religion, including Christianity, as anti-reason and anti-science.

Sadly, far too many Christians continue to accept the false assertion that Christianity and science are at war with each other, or else that they operate in entirely different and wholly disconnected spheres. In some Christian circles, asking hard questions about the Bible is frowned on, if not explicitly, then implicitly. There are certain questions you just don't ask. The implication that many, particularly young people, take away is this: Don't ask hard questions. Don't doubt. Don't think or trust in reason. Just believe.

Tragically, many Christians believe the strange idea that their so-called "faith" somehow makes Christianity true. The object of their faith isn't the objective reality of God or the truthfulness of the Bible, but faith itself. They believe in the so-called "power of belief."

Postmodernism rejects objective truth in favor of personal and private views of "truth." This has had a disastrous impact on the concept of faith. In our postmodern world, faith becomes personal and subjective. "If your faith works for you, fine." It can be "true" for you. Such a subjective faith doesn't require reason or evidence. It might even be opposed to reason or evidence. Subjective faith lives only in the mind of the "believer." It is a private faith, not a public reality.

Discussion Questions
- How does the redefinition of faith differ from the true definition? Discuss all that has changed.
- In what ways have you seen or experienced the redefinition of faith?
- What are some of the social and cultural changes in which the redefinition of faith has resulted?

Personal Reflection and Application
Next week at home, take time to reflect on these areas of application. Read the questions and write down your responses.

Reflect on your faith in God and the trustworthiness of his Word in Scripture.

QUESTION: To what degree is your faith based on an honest exploration of the evidence for the existence of God, the reliability and truthfulness of the Bible, and the historical reality of Jesus and his death and resurrection?

If you have questions or doubts about these things, don't bury or ignore them. Express them in the form of questions, honestly seek answers to them, and commit to following the evidence wherever it leads.

QUESTION: If you claim faith in Jesus, does it go beyond "saving faith?" Describe how your faith affects all areas of your life—your work, finances, relationships, and daily decisions.

Many Christians claim to have faith in Jesus as their personal Savior but not as their supreme authority. The truth is that Jesus doesn't give us this choice. If he is your Savior, he also demands your complete allegiance in total surrender over every part of your life, just as Jesus himself modeled for us (Luke 22:42).

Anything short of this is not genuine faith in Jesus. Your choices and actions will prove what you place your ultimate trust in. People will see the difference between putting total trust in Jesus or putting it elsewhere.

QUESTION: Consider your own trustworthiness or faithfulness. Examine your relationships with friends, spouse, family members, business relationships, and coworkers. How would they rate your integrity and trustworthiness? Do you keep your vows? Do your words and actions align?

A life (and a whole society) built on the worship of the One True God of the Bible has high levels of personal trust because God is utterly trustworthy and true, and when we worship him we become "like him" (1 John 3:2).

Today there is a profound breakdown of trust in our culture, reflected in everything from high divorce rates to soaring levels of cynicism in our institutions. Many people can't name a single person they can genuinely trust. Rebuilding trust must begin with each of us. We may be unable to change the culture, but we can change our relationships. We can change our family, church, sports team, and office environment. This is where it begins. You can rebuild trust in our society by being a faithful, trustworthy person in your circles of influence. How? Not in your strength, but by trusting entirely in Jesus Christ. He will give you the power to do this because you will see that he is altogether trustworthy.

Concluding Thoughts

It isn't an overstatement to say that the entire message of the Bible can be summarized as follows: *Trust God.* Trust his promises. He will never let you down.

"Biblical faith is not blind trust in the face of contrary evidence, not an unknowable 'leap in the dark'; rather, [it] is a confident trust in the eternal God who is all-powerful, infinitely wise, eternally trustworthy—the God who has revealed himself in his word and in the person of Jesus Christ, whose promises have proven true fromgeneration to generation, and who will 'never leave nor forsake' his own (Hebrews 13:5)."[7]

RECOMMENDED RESOURCES

Books

- *The Case for Christ: A Journalist's Personal Investigation of the Evidence for Jesus* by Lee Strobel (Zondervan, 2016)
- *Evidence That Demands a Verdict: Life-Changing Truth for a Skeptical World* by Josh McDowell and Sean McDowell (Thomas Nelson, 2017)
- *Unearthing the Bible: 101 Archaeological Discoveries That Bring the Bible to Life* by Titus Kennedy (Harvest House Publishers, 2020)
- *Is Atheism Dead?* by Eric Metaxas (Salem Books, 2021)
- *Unbelievable: Why, After Ten Years of Talking with Atheists, I'm Still a Christian* by Justin Brierley (SPCK, 2017)
- *Cold-Case Christianity: A Homicide Detective Investigates the Claims of the Gospels* by J. Warner Wallace (David C. Cook, 2013)
- *The Reason for God: Belief in an Age of Skepticism* by Timothy Keller (Penguin Books, 2008)

Video

- The Bible Project: *The Reason You Can Trust God (Even When It Seems Risky)*

BEAUTY

What is beauty? How do you define it?

Many people think of beauty as something nice but not essential. It's a matter of personal taste. It's "in the eye of the beholder."

But is there more to beauty? Is there an objective reality to beauty that goes beyond our tastes and opinions?

Is beauty essential for human flourishing? Is it essential for faithful Christian life and ministry?

This week we're reading Chapter 9, "Beauty," in *10 Words to Heal Our Broken World* by Scott David Allen.

PERSONAL BIBLE STUDY: *BEAUTY*

Before You Begin

In the space below write a concise, dictionary-style definition of beauty from your current understanding without consulting sources such as a dictionary, the internet, or another person. The purpose is to record your current understanding and see how it changes due to this study.

BIBLE STUDY

Read the following passages and prayerfully respond to the question below.

From Zion, perfect in beauty, God shines forth. (Psalm 50:2)

One thing I ask from the LORD, this only do I seek: that I may dwell in the house of the LORD all the days of my life, to gaze on the beauty of the LORD and to seek him in his temple. (Psalm 27:4)

LORD my God, you are very great; you are clothed with splendor and majesty. The LORD wraps himself in light as with a garment; he stretches out the heavens like a tent and lays the beams of his upper chambers on their waters. He makes the clouds his chariot and rides on the wings of the wind. He makes winds his messengers, flames of fire his servants. (Psalm 104:1–4)

Holy, holy, holy is the LORD Almighty; the whole earth is full of his glory. (Isaiah 6:3).

QUESTION: According to these passages, what is the source of beauty?

Reflect on these quotes from the *10 Words* book:
Beauty finds its source in God, the "perfection of beauty" (Psalm 50:2). He is glorious, flawless, and morally perfect. We see the perfection of his beauty in his holiness, lovingkindness, and mercy. We see it in Jesus's

tender compassion when he touched a man with leprosy and healed him. Most sublimely, we see it in Jesus's breathtaking love, displayed in his sacrificial death on the cross, giving himself completely so that we might live.

Words synonymous with beautiful *include* delightful, sublime, radiant, perfect, glorious, flawless, *and* exquisite. *Antonyms include* hideous, unsightly, repulsive, foul, vile, ghastly, *and* loathsome.

Read the following passages and prayerfully respond to the questions below.

In the beginning God created the heavens and the earth. (Genesis 1:1)

This is what God the Lord says—the Creator of the heavens, who stretches them out, who spreads out the earth with all that springs from it, who gives breath to its people, and life to those who walk on it. (Isaiah 42:5)

Through him all things were made; without him nothing was made that has been made. In him was life, and that life was the light of all mankind. The light shines in the darkness, and the darkness has not overcome it. (John 1:3–5)

God saw all that he had made, and it was very good (Genesis 1:31)

The Lord God made all kinds of trees grow out of the ground—trees that were pleasing to the eye and good for food. (Genesis 2:9)

I praise you, for I am fearfully and wonderfully made; your works are wonderful, I know that full well. (Psalm 139:14)

How many are your works, Lord! In wisdom you made them all; the earth is full of your creatures. There is the sea, vast and spacious, teeming with creatures beyond number—living things both large and small. (Psalm 104:24–25)

He has made everything beautiful in its time (Ecclesiastes 3:11)

QUESTION: From these passages, how has God expressed beauty through his creation?

QUESTION: How do you experience beauty in creation? Write down a few thoughts or experiences that quickly come to mind.

Reflect on this quote from the *10 Words* book:

We experience the perfection of God's beauty in the magnificent artistry of creation. People everywhere experience the beauty of creation in ways big and small, in shapes, colors, sounds, forms, designs, and patterns. In mountain vistas and the brilliant colors of a sunrise. In a snow crystal's intricate, delicate pattern. In a child's eye. In the incredible order and symmetry of the DNA molecule or a distant galaxy. Even in something as simple as a carefully tilled field or a well-tended garden. We also experience beauty in cleanness, order, and purity. We recognize beauty in a well-kept and tastefully decorated room in a way we don't when that room is dirty and disheveled. We recognize beauty in a crystal clear mountain stream in a way that we don't when that stream is clogged with trash.

Read the following passages and prayerfully respond to the questions below.

O worship the LORD in the beauty of holiness. (Psalm 96:9 KJV21)

Your beauty should not come from outward adornment, such as elaborate hairstyles and the wearing of gold jewelry or fine clothes. Rather, it should be that of your inner self, the unfading beauty of a gentle and quiet spirit, which is of great worth in God's sight. (1 Peter 3:3–4)

Whatever is true, whatever is noble, whatever is right, whatever is pure, whatever is lovely, whatever is admirable— if anything is excellent or praiseworthy—think about such things. (Philippians 4:8)

QUESTION: How do these passages describe beauty?

QUESTION: How have you experienced the inward or invisible beauty of God's moral perfection or human virtue?

Reflect on these quotes from the *10 Words* book:

Not all beauty is external and experienced through our senses. There is also an invisible, inward beauty we experience in moral virtues such as kindness, compassion, love, sacrifice, courage, or inner strength. There is a deep connection between beauty and goodness, or moral virtue. Psalm 96:9, for example, describes God's moral perfection as "beautiful."

Because beauty is sourced in God—in his character and creation—it is an objective reality regardless of our subjective feelings about it. In this way beauty is the same as truth and goodness, which are also universal, objective realities rooted in God's character.

Read the following passages and prayerfully respond to the questions below.

The heavens declare the glory of God; the skies proclaim the work of his hands. Day after day they pour forth speech; night after night they reveal knowledge. They have no speech; they use no words; no sound is heard from them. Yet their voice goes out into all the earth, their words to the ends of the world. (Psalm 19:1–4)

"Consider how the wild flowers grow. They do not labor or spin. Yet I tell you, not even Solomon in all his splendor was dressed like one of these." (Luke 12:27)

"Ask the animals, and they will teach you; or the birds in the sky, and they will tell you; or speak to the earth, and it will teach you; or let the fish in the sea inform you. Which of all these does not know that the hand of the LORD has done this? In his hand is the life of every creature and the breath of all mankind." (Job 12:7–9)

God's invisible qualities—his eternal power and divine nature—have been clearly seen, being understood from what has been made, so that people are without excuse. (Romans 1:20)

QUESTION: How does creation reveal God's existence and his divine nature?

QUESTION: What do we learn about the First Artist from his magnificent artistry in creation?

Reflect on these quotes from the _10 Words_ book:

"Beauty is God's first, last, and most effective messenger. We learn that the world is good and orderly because of the beauty of [Creation], which we only later come to understand intellectually . . . we come to know God through His divine artistry."—Jerry Root and Stan Guthrie[1]

Contrary to much modern thinking, people are not disembodied brains, like some kind of mechanistic Artificial Intelligence system, but embodied human beings made to experience and engage in the full range of God's created order. Beauty isn't an optional, decorative "add-on" for human flourishing and knowledge of truth and goodness. It is a moral necessity.

As image-bearers of God, the source of all beauty, human beings are drawn naturally to beauty. There is a strong relationship between beauty and delight, joy, or enjoyment. In the words of the English poet John Keats, "A thing of beauty is a joy forever." Beauty draws us, while the ugly, foul, and vile repulse us.

Consider the power of beauty. It communicates to us deeply, touching the depths of our soul. It arrests our attention, prompts tears of joy, and engenders feelings of awe that cannot be described adequately by mere words.

"Beauty is the gateway to goodness and truth."—Elizabeth Lev[2]

Read the following passages and prayerfully respond to the questions below.

The LORD God took the man and put him in the garden of Eden to work it and keep it. (Genesis 2:15 ESV)

[God] has filled him [Bezalel, the craftsman who oversaw the construction of the tabernacle] with the Spirit of God, with skill, with intelligence, with knowledge, and with all craftsmanship, to devise artistic designs, to work in gold and silver and bronze. (Exodus 35:31–32 ESV)

"You have an abundance of workmen: stonecutters, masons, carpenters, and all kinds of craftsmen without number, skilled in working gold, silver, bronze, and iron. Arise and work! The LORD be with you!" (1 Chronicles 22:15–16 ESV)

[King Uzziah] built towers in the wilderness and cut out many cisterns, for he had large herds, both in the Shephelah and in the plain, and he had farmers and vinedressers in the hills and in the fertile lands, for he loved the soil. (2 Chronicles 26:10)

Do you see a man skillful in his work? He will stand before kings; he will not stand before obscure men. (Proverbs 22:29 ESV)

Whatever you do, work heartily, as for the Lord and not for men, knowing that from the Lord you will receive the inheritance as your reward. (Colossians 3:23–24 ESV)

Praise him with tambourine and dance; praise him with strings and pipe! (Psalm 150:4)

Let them praise his name with dancing, making melody to him with tambourine and lyre! (Psalm 149:3)

QUESTION: Beauty is sourced in God and his creation, but according to these passages, where else is it sourced?

QUESTION: What are some simple (and not so simple) ways you can produce beauty through your creative endeavors?

Reflect on these quotes from the *10 Words* book:

Beauty is sourced in God, but also in the human spirit. We, too, can create beauty because we bear God's image. In the words of the great novelist J. R. R. Tolkien, "Beginning with what God has provided, man can actually make new things. A composer can create a symphony that no one has ever before heard. A painter can create a painting that no eye has ever before seen. A poet can write a poem that no one has ever read."[3] To experience, delight in, and create beauty are significant parts of being human. As Darrow Miller said, "Beauty is a necessity for life." It is essential for human flourishing.

The beauty we create begins with God, the source of all that is beautiful, and our discovery and imitation of his character and creative genius. As we carefully and deeply reflect on God's character, revealed Word, and creation, we can discover or derive ideas and principles that we apply to our creative work. In doing so we imitate God in our creative endeavors and create more beauty, which pleases God and is a form of worship. The process begins and ends with God.

"An author should never conceive of himself as bringing into existence beauty or wisdom which did not exist before, but simply and solely as trying to embody in terms of his own art some reflection of that eternal Beauty and Wisdom."—C. S. Lewis[4]

The Hebrew word Avodah can be translated as either "work" or "worship." When done in imitation of God's beauty, our handiwork gives God honor and glory.

LEARNING TOGETHER: *BEAUTY*
Welcome and Opening Prayer

Opening Discussion
Discuss together what you learned about beauty during your personal study. What ideas stood out to you? How did God speak to you through the Scriptures?

Watch the Video and Discuss the Questions Below
Note: You'll find the "beauty" video at 10WordsBook.org.
- What insights did you gain from the video about beauty?
- What insights did you gain about the redefinition of beauty?

Definitions and Discussion
Read the two definitions and quotes below. Discuss the contemporary redefinition of beauty and its cultural consequences.

BEAUTY

A combination of qualities present in a thing or person, both externally and internally, that gives joy and deep satisfaction. Beauty can move us deeply and fill us with awe and wonder. Because God is its ultimate source, beauty has an objective reality that transcends personal tastes. Along with truth and goodness, it is considered one of three such "transcendentals."

BEAUTY REDEFINED

A combination of aesthetic qualities that appeal to one's personal, subjective senses or tastes. Beauty is entirely a matter of personal preference and individual expression.

Reflect on these quotes from the *10 Words* book:

Today most people think of beauty as something entirely personal and subjective. We've reduced beauty to an outlet for individual expression or aesthetic tastes, with many contemporary artists "merely using their art to make statements, often for nothing more than shock value." [5]

We no longer believe that beauty is an objective, transcendent reality; instead, we decide what is beautiful. As the British philosopher David Hume said, "Beauty in things exists merely in the mind which contemplates them." [6] *We no longer see beauty as a moral necessity; instead, we see it as an optional decoration, ornament, or accessory. In the United States the priority is on the pragmatic. The essential questions are "Does it work?" and "Is it functional?" Seldom do we ask, "Is it beautiful?"*

Beginning in late 19th-century France, a group dubbed the Impressionists rebelled against classical standards of beauty rooted in Christian ideas and principles. The movement marked a turning point in Western art and creativity. These artistic revolutionaries rejected objective, transcendent standards for beauty but offered nothing to replace them beyond individual preference and personal expression.

This rebellion against classical standards has ripples that extend far beyond the fine arts. Today they shape how we think about creativity in nearly every realm of human endeavor, from urban planning to architecture to literature, music, education, and beyond. We see the bitter fruits everywhere. Many of our major cities are now filled with graffiti, their streets littered with trash and even human excrement. Abandoned buildings with boarded-up windows line streets—a previous generation's magnificent architecture and urban design thoroughly despoiled.

When we reject God, we lose not only objective truth and goodness, but objective beauty as well. Much of today's creative expression is little more than open rebellion against God, the source of all beauty. As a result it moves toward the hideous, repulsive, repellent, and grotesque. Beauty fades away, and we are left with only ugliness. That is a world in which no human being should ever want to live.

How has the evangelical church responded? Sadly, not by vigorously defending and preserving the classical standard of beauty and its magnificent legacy but mainly by ignoring it and dismissing beauty as an unimportant subject.

The evangelical church has largely lost the biblical truth about beauty. Instead, we've largely absorbed the false modern and postmodern ideas about it. Today most Christians believe that beauty is entirely subjective, a matter of personal taste and nothing more. They have lost any sense of beauty's objective, transcendent nature, or they simply ignore beauty or act as if it doesn't matter. At most, beauty is viewed as an ornamental add-on but not an essential part of Christian faithfulness and witness.

Discussion Questions

- How does the redefinition of beauty differ from the true definition? Discuss all that has changed.
- In what ways have you seen or experienced the redefinition of beauty?
- What are some of the social and cultural changes in which the redefinition of beauty has resulted?

Personal Reflection and Application

Next week at home, take time to reflect on these areas of application. Read the questions and write down your responses.

As followers of Jesus, the source of all beauty, let's do what we can to recover a proper, biblical understanding of beauty. As Christ's ambassadors, our calling is to represent him truthfully. We can't do that without showing forth his beauty in all of its radiant splendor.

Consider your assumptions about beauty.

QUESTION: Before going through this session, did you see beauty as something subjective—in the eye of the beholder—or objective, rooted in God's character and creation? How did your thinking change as a result of working through this session?

Most Christians understand that we are to speak the truth and reject lies. We know that we are to do what is morally right and reject what is sinful and unjust. But do we know equally well that we are to create and celebrate beauty and reject the hideous—and that this is just as important?

QUESTION: On a scale of 1 to 10, with one being "not important at all" and 10 being "essential," how would you rate your understanding of the importance of beauty to a faithful Christian life and to communicating truthfully about Jesus Christ?

If your answer is on the low end of the spectrum, I invite you to change the way you think about beauty. As we've said in previous chapters, repentance (Greek *metanoia*) literally means "to change your mind." Change the way you think. Take your thoughts captive and make them obedient to Christ (2 Corinthians 10:5). Recognize and embrace the truth that beauty is as central to God's essence as truth, goodness, or moral perfection. To treat beauty as optional is to betray a profoundly faulty understanding of God. If our knowledge of God is defective, so will be our witness of him in the world. Beauty may be the most potent and strategic gospel witness in this generation.

If beauty is a moral necessity, how can we bring more of it into our lives?

QUESTION: How can you bring more order and beauty into your personal spaces, including your home, apartment, or other property?

QUESTION: How can you bring more beauty into your life, including your body and personal hygiene?

QUESTION: How can you cultivate the inner beauty of your character as expressed in your relationships with others?

Jordan Peterson famously taught young people that, to bring order into their lives, they should start by "making their bed." That's good advice that applies to beauty as well. Create beauty in your personal spaces, such as your apartment, bedroom, or home. Put things away, hang up your clothes, clean, and set your place in order. Make this a habit and part of your routine.

Do you have a yard or garden overrun with weeds and plants that need trimming? Work to transform your outdoor spaces, no matter how small, into something beautiful.

Are you caring for your body well? What improvements can you make here? Remember, too, that genuine beauty is both inner and outer. Are you cultivating the inner beauty the apostle Peter spoke of? This is a spirit of gentleness, humility, and genuine love for your family, friends, and neighbors.

God's magnificent creation is a source of immense beauty. It draws people powerfully to God, so we should care for it. But sadly, this simple idea has become controversial in the church. Many Christians understandably react against environmentalists who often operate from neo-pagan and anti-human assumptions and worship "nature" as a god. As a result, many of us simply choose to avoid the subject. But reacting against non-Christian ideologies or movements isn't helpful. Instead, let's recover a genuine ethic of creation rooted in some basic biblical principles we all can agree on.

QUESTION: What are some practical ways by which you can care for and beautify God's creation—in your neighborhood or city and in the land, water, and air around you?

If your vocation involves creative work, such as that done by artisans, filmmakers, designers, musicians, chefs, photographers, writers, and artists, you have a vital role in God's kingdom.

In recent years Christian artists and creators have earned a reputation (whether fairly or not) for inferior work that copies trends in pop culture and adds a "Christianizing" element, such as a gospel message or biblical themes. With a few exceptions, most leading writers, painters, novelists, musicians, composers, filmmakers, and architects are non-Christians. But we, of all people, should be producing works of the highest quality and most excellent beauty.

QUESTION: Do you understand that your creative work is a form of worship? How can you honor and glorify God more effectively through your creative endeavors?

QUESTION: If you are a pastor, how can you better teach, encourage, and inspire the creative individuals in your congregation to do their "utmost for his highest?"

Concluding Thoughts

"Beauty has a unique power to do something that only it can do: generate longing, a longing that is satisfied supremely in the Source of all created beauties, Jesus Christ"—David Taylor[7]

RECOMMENDED RESOURCES

Books

- *A Call for Balladeers: Pursuing Art and Beauty for the Discipling of Nations* by Darrow L. Miller (YWAM Publishing, 2022)
- *Tree and Leaf: Including Mythopoeia* by J. R. R. Tolkien (Tolkien, International Edition, 2001)
- *The Evidential Power of Beauty: Science and Theology Meet* by Thomas Dubay (Ignatius Press, 1999)
- *Art and Faith: A Theology of Making* by Makoto Fujimura (Yale University Press, 2021)
- *Art and the Bible* by Francis Schaeffer (InterVarsity Press 2nd Edition, 2006)

Videos

- *Bishop Barron on Evangelizing Through Beauty youtube.com/ watch?v=bBMOwZFpZX0*
- *Robert Florczak, Why Is Modern Art So Bad?*
- *prageru.com/video/why-is-modern-art-so-bad*

LOVE

How do you define love?

We use this word all the time. It is everywhere in our culture. We hear people say, "I love pizza," "I love my wife," or "I love to ski."

We see it all over social media: the hashtag "Love Wins." The hashtag "Love is Love." It's the subject of countless films, songs, and novels.

In the Bible we read that God is love and that we are to "love our neighbor as ourselves."

For a word we use so much, *love* is hard to define.

Do we really know what love means?

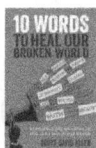 This week we're reading Chapter 10, "Love," in *10 Words to Heal Our Broken World* by Scott David Allen.

PERSONAL BIBLE STUDY: *LOVE*

Before You Begin

In the space below write a concise, dictionary-style definition of love from your current understanding without consulting sources such as a dictionary, the internet, or another person. The purpose is to record your current understanding and see how it changes due to this study.

BIBLE STUDY
Read the following passages and prayerfully respond to the question below.

Love is from God . . . whoever loves has been born of God and knows God . . . because God is love. (1 John 4:7–8 ESV)

"Love the Lord your God with all your heart and with all your soul and with all your mind. This is the first and greatest commandment." (Matthew 22:36–38 ESV)

Love is the fulfillment of the law. (Romans 13:10)

If I speak in the tongues of men and of angels, but have not love, I am a noisy gong or a clanging cymbal. And if I have prophetic powers, and understand all mysteries and all knowledge, and if I have all faith, so as to remove mountains, but have not love, I am nothing. If I give away all I have, and if I deliver up my body to be burned, but have not love, I gain nothing. (1 Corinthians 13:1–3, ESV)

And now these three remain: faith, hope, and love. But the greatest of these is love. (1 Corinthians 13:13)

The fruit of the Spirit is love. (Galatians 5:22)

For God so loved the world that he gave his one and only Son, that whoever believes in him shall not perish but have eternal life. (John 3:16)

QUESTION: What do these passages reveal about the centrality of love in the Bible?

Reflect on these quotes from the *10 Words* book:

Of all the words explored in this book, love is the most important because it is the vital center of God's character. The apostle John used the word love to describe the essence of God's nature. There is no more critical word—no more important concept—than love, so nothing could be more important than understanding it as clearly as possible.

The word love can be challenging to define because we use it to describe our feelings about objects as varied as pizza, beautiful sunsets, a spouse, or God. To make sense of this, consider that when we say "I love pizza," we use the word in a shallow but not necessarily false way. However, we are in much deeper waters when we speak about God's love for us, our love for our children, or what it means to love our enemies.

Read the following passages and prayerfully respond to the question below.

[God] will take great delight in you; in his love he will no longer rebuke you, but will rejoice over you with singing. (Zephaniah 3:17)

Let him kiss me with the kisses of his mouth—for your love is more delightful than wine. (Song of Songs 1:2)

The LORD appeared to us in the past, saying: "I have loved you with an everlasting love; I have drawn you with unfailing kindness." (Jeremiah 31:3)

[Nothing] in all creation, will be able to separate us from the love of God in Christ Jesus our Lord. (see Romans 8:39)

This is how we know what love is: Jesus Christ laid down his life for us. (1 John 3:16)

This is love: not that we loved God, but that he loved us and sent his Son as an atoning sacrifice for our sins. (1 John 4:10)

QUESTION: Love is a multi-faceted concept that involves both feelings and actions. What are some of the facets of love revealed in the passages above?

Reflect on these quotes from the *10 Words* book:

Like a priceless diamond, love has various facets. These facets can appear contradictory, but each is essential and overlapping, and together they form a magnificent whole. Love describes things we enjoy or delight in. It can also describe affection for people we treasure and long to be near. Going deeper, it involves promises of commitment and fidelity. At the deepest level, love transcends personal desires and involves pursuing another person's highest good, even at a significant cost. This selflessness is what makes love so beautiful and powerful.

Some claim that biblical love has nothing to do with feelings or emotions. We often hear that "love is not a feeling but an act of the will." There is truth in this. Love sometimes requires hard choices and sacrifices, even regarding our enemies. Choices that don't depend on our feelings. But even then, joy will surely follow actions done in love (Hebrews 12:2). Our well-intentioned attempts to separate love from emotions such as joy and delight damage the richness of the concept.

In the Old Testament the Hebrew word hesed is translated into English as "love" or "lovingkindness." It appears 246 times in the

Hebrew Scriptures. Hesed is synonymous with goodness, kindness, faithfulness, mercy, and compassion. God's hesed is unchanging, consistent, steadfast, and unfailing. As the repeated refrain of Psalm 136 declares, "His love [hesed] endures forever."

In the New Testament the most common Greek word translated into English as "love" is agape, which appears more than 200 times. Agape love is a love of choice that requires faithfulness, commitment, and sacrifice without expecting anything in return. It is the love shown by the Good Samaritan to the man beaten and left dying on the side of the road (Luke 10:25–37). It describes Christ's sacrificial service for fallen, broken people, most fully displayed through his atoning death on the cross.

Read the following passages and prayerfully respond to the questions below.

Dear friends, let us love one another, for love is from God. Everyone who loves has been born of God and knows God . . . because God is love. (1 John 4:7–8)

"Father, I [Jesus] want those you have given me to be with me where I am, and to see my glory, the glory you have given me because you loved me before the creation of the world." (John 17:24)

The Lord came down in the cloud and stood there with [Moses] and proclaimed his name, the Lord. And he passed in front of Moses, proclaiming, "The Lord, the Lord, the compassionate and gracious God, slow to anger, abounding in love and faithfulness, maintaining love to thousands, and forgiving wickedness, rebellion and sin." (Exodus 34:5–7)

QUESTION: According to John 17:24, what existed "before the creation of the world"?

QUESTION: According to these passages, what is the source of love?

Reflect on these quotes from the *10 Words* book:

Where does love come from? Not from the often-selfish character of the pagan gods, such as those from ancient Greece or Rome, or in the lives and teachings of the Buddha or Muhammad. It is entirely absent from the secular, materialistic worldview rooted in Darwinism and the "survival of the fittest" or in the Marxist quest for power and control. Love finds its source in God and nowhere else. We would have no concept of it apart from him.

God is not an impersonal power, force, or idea. He is a person. To love someone and be loved in return are characteristics of free, personal beings, which is what God is. Because God exists at the foundation of all things, the universe is ultimately personal, and love is the most elemental reality of all. Secularism is a lie. The most fundamental reality is not matter, energy, or the will to power—it is love.

Some falsely believe that God created human beings because he was lonely and needed someone to love. The truth is that complete love and fullness of joy existed among the three persons of the Trinity—

Father, Son, and Holy Spirit—before the creation of humanity. At creation this love and joy overflowed to God's image-bearers so that we, in turn, could extend it to others.

"God loves from an outpouring of who He is."—Alyssa Roat[1]

There is no more important truth than this. God loves you more than you could ever hope or fully realize. God, your Maker, treasures you and cares deeply about every part of your life. He delights in you and longs to be near you in a deep, personal, and eternal relationship. He views you as immensely valuable—so valuable that he was willing to lay down his life for you. When you grasp this, it will transform you and become the bedrock of your identity.

Read the following passages and prayerfully respond to the question below.

Jacob was in love with Rachel . . . Jacob served [Laban, Rachel's father] seven years to get Rachel, but they seemed like only a few days to him because of his love for her. (Genesis 29:18, 20)

Jonathan became one in spirit with David, and he loved him as himself . . . And Jonathan made a covenant with David because he loved him as himself. (1 Samuel 18:1–3)

You, LORD, have made me joyful by what You have done, I will sing for joy over the works of Your hands. (Psalm 92:4 NASB)

[Jesus said to his disciples,] "A new command I give you. Love one another. As I have loved you, so you must love one another." (John 13:34)

QUESTION: The passages above refer to human love. Where does our capacity to love come from, and why is it essential for human flourishing?

Reflect on these quotes from the *10 Words* book:

Just as love is central to God's character, it is also central to ours. As image-bearers of God we are hard-wired for love. We all experience joy and delight in God's magnificent creation. We love to walk on a beach at sunset. We love to enjoy a delicious meal with family and friends. We love beautiful music. We also experience love in our most fundamental relationships: marriage, family, and close friendships. Loving others and being loved by them is essential for human flourishing. Without love human existence would be virtually impossible. Life would be empty and meaningless.

The fall of humankind profoundly distorts how we love. We love money or power more than people made in God's image. We love ourselves more than others. We often practice the opposite of love in our fallen, selfish condition. We break our promises, divorce our spouses, neglect our children, and seek our self-interest above the good of others. Yet people worldwide and throughout history have experienced love imperfectly and incompletely. It is part of our imago Dei. It gives our lives meaning, purpose, and belonging. We long for the love of another, and we find joy and meaning in our lives by loving others.

Read the following passages and prayerfully respond to the question below.

Teacher, which is the greatest commandment in the Law?"

Jesus replied: "'Love the Lord your God with all your heart

and with all your soul and with all your mind.' This is the first and greatest commandment. And the second is like it: 'Love your neighbor as yourself.' All the Law and the Prophets hang on these two commandments." (Matthew 22:36–40)

"Anyone who loves their father or mother more than me is not worthy of me; anyone who loves their son or daughter more than me is not worthy of me. Whoever does not take up their cross and follow me is not worthy of me." (Matthew 10:37–38)

QUESTION: What do these passages teach about love's proper order of priority?

Reflect on these quotes from the *10 Words* book:
The Bible has a great deal to say about loving relationships. At creation God established four fundamental relationships common to all people: our relationships with God, ourselves, others, and creation. As Augustine taught in the fourth century, there is a God-ordained order of priority to these relationships based on value or worth. Put simply, the greater the worth, the greater the priority to love.

God is at the pinnacle. He is supremely worthy of our love and devotion as the Holy, Almighty Creator of all. Next, in order of value, come God's image-bearers, including ourselves. All people, whether male or female, rich or poor, powerful or vulnerable, born or unborn, regardless of age or ethnicity, are precious to God. Last, in order of value, comes the stuff of the created world, including the physical environment, plants, animals, and things we create, like money, cars, homes, businesses, and everything else.

Our relationships thrive when we understand and respect this God-established order and prioritize our love accordingly. However, when we neglect this order, things start to crumble. Disordered love is a hideous counterfeit. It morphs into destructive idolatry and becomes a source of evil.

Our fallen hearts still love, but they reject God and replace him with the "idols" of money, fame, sex, power, narcotics, hedonistic pleasures, or even our spouse or children. These idols may satisfy us momentarily, but ultimately they will leave us empty, frustrated, and often depressed. Why? Because they are incapable of satisfying our deepest needs. Only God can. To paraphrase Blaise Pascal, "There is a God-shaped vacuum in the heart of every person which cannot be filled by any created thing, but only by God the Creator, made known through Jesus Christ."[2]

"If our hearts are right, we love God above all things as the source of all that is good, desirable, and excellent. In Him, we find our greatest joy."—Noah Webster[3]

Read the following passages and prayerfully respond to the questions below.

[Jesus said,] "I love the Father and do exactly what my Father has commanded me." (John 14:31)

"Whoever has my commands and keeps them is the one who loves me." (John 14:21)

Whoever claims to love God yet hates a brother or sister is a liar. For whoever does not love their brother and sister, whom they have seen, cannot love God, whom they have not seen. And he has given us this command: Anyone who loves God must also love their brother and sister. (1 John 4:20–21)

The entire law is fulfilled in keeping this one command: Love your neighbor as yourself. (Galatians 5:14)

QUESTION: According to these passages, how do we demonstrate love for God?

QUESTION: Why is "loving our neighbor" so crucial in the Bible?

QUESTION: Read the Parable of the Good Samaritan in Luke 10:25–37. How does Jesus define "neighbor," and what does love for one's neighbor mean specifically?

Reflect on these quotes from the *10 Words* book:

We demonstrate our love and devotion to Jesus by obeying his commands in the same way that Jesus demonstrated his love for the Father through obedience to his commands. That obedience took Jesus to the cross for the sake of love. Our obedience to Christ demands that we love others in the same way.

The Bible teaches that we are to love God first and people second, but we express our love for God by loving others because they are made in his divine image. Loving God and loving our neighbor are closely intertwined in Scripture.

The love demonstrated by the Good Samaritan crossed lines of ethnicity and hostility. It was compassionate, gracious, costly, sacrificial, unconditional, unreciprocated, and undeserved. This is exactly how Jesus loved us. He saw our broken condition. It filled his great heart with compassion and moved him to costly action on our behalf. He drew near to us in the incarnation, entering our suffering and ultimately taking the punishment we deserved upon himself, all to reconcile us to God.

Read the following passages and prayerfully respond to the question below.

God demonstrates his own love for us in this: While we were still sinners, Christ died for us. (Romans 5:8)

While we were God's enemies, we were reconciled to him through the death of his Son. (Romans 5:10)

You have heard that it was said, "Love your neighbor and hate your enemy." But I [Jesus] tell you, love your enemies and pray for those who persecute you, that you may be children of your Father in heaven. He causes his sun to rise on the evil and the good, and sends rain on the righteous and the unrighteous. If you love those who love you, what reward will you get? Are not even the tax collectors doing that? And if you greet only your own people, what are you doing more than others? Do not even pagans do that? Be perfect, therefore, as your heavenly Father is perfect." (Matthew 5:43–48)

QUESTION: The Bible teaches that we are to love our neighbor, which extends even to our enemies—those who actively oppose us and seek our harm. From the passages above, what reasons are given for why we should do something so radical?

Reflect on these quotes from the *10 Words* book:

We are never more Christlike than when we love our enemies, and this opens the door to experiencing God's pleasure like nothing else. There is no greater joy than hearing our heavenly Father say these words in response to our obedience: "Well done, good and faithful servant" (Matthew 25:23).

To choose to love someone who has harmed us deeply when emotions such as anger, bitterness, resentment, and vengefulness are so strong that we feel helpless against their power is nothing short of a miracle. But when such miracles occur, the watching world is confronted with God's reality and power. The miracle of loving our enemies is a brilliant light shining in the dark. It unleashes incredible transformational power—the power to overcome evil (Romans 12:21). When we witness such transformation or are privileged to play a role in it through our obedience, we experience intense joy.

Read the following passage and prayerfully respond to the questions below.

The LORD did not set his affection on you [Israel] and choose you because you were more numerous than other peoples, for you were the fewest of all peoples. But it was because the LORD loved you and kept the oath he swore to your ancestors. (Deuteronomy 7:7–8)

QUESTION: According to this passage, why does God love Israel and, by extension, his church (see Romans 11:1–24)?

QUESTION: Why is free choice essential to love?

Reflect on these quotes from the *10 Words* book:

Freedom is not just a component of love but is an integral part. Love, by its very nature, must be freely chosen. It cannot be imposed, programmed, or coerced. Without the element of choice, love loses its essence.

At the center of God's nature are love and freedom. Because God is free, no one compels him to do anything against his will. He loves us because he chooses to. We see this throughout the Bible. God chooses people and loves them, not because they are particularly lovable or worthy of God's special attention but simply because he chooses them.

As God's image-bearers, we, too, can freely choose. We are not robots or machines. God made us free to relate to him and others in love. While someone may force us to do things against our will, loving will never be one of those things. Unless love is given freely, it is not love.

Read the following passages and prayerfully respond to the question below.

"[God] does not leave the guilty unpunished; he punishes the children and their children for the sin of the parents to the third and fourth generation." (Exodus 34:7).

He was pierced for our transgressions, he was crushed for our iniquities; the punishment that brought us peace was on him, and by his wounds we are healed. (Isaiah 53:5)

The Lord disciplines the one he loves, and he chastens everyone he accepts as his son. (Hebrews 12:6)

Whoever spares the rod hates their children, but the one who loves their children is careful to discipline them. (Proverbs 13:24)

QUESTION: Are love and justice (specifically judgment of wrongdoing, punishment, and discipline) contradictory in the Bible? Explain your answer.

Reflect on these quotes from the *10 Words* book:

Love and justice coexist in God's character and in human relationships. While God loves sinners, he hates the evil and injustice they commit and cannot overlook it in his moral perfection or brush it off as no big deal. Injustice is intolerable to God because it harms the people he loves. The same applies to us. We, too, seek justice when someone harms a person we love who is under our care and protection.

It is not loving to allow a sinner to continue on his sinful path without consequences. We must never sacrifice justice, which God loves, or enable evil, which God hates, in the name of love.

The Bible frequently discusses the relationship between love, discipline, and punishment. Our fallen, sinful nature enables all kinds of wrongdoing, ultimately harming us and others. Those in positions of authority express love by caring enough to attempt to correct the evil through discipline and punishment, not by ignoring wrongdoing and the harm it causes.

Ultimately, God's love and justice reach their full expression in the cross of Jesus Christ. Justice, because sin and human evil stirred God's holy wrath. Punishment and payment for that evil were required for justice to prevail. Love, because Jesus took the punishment we deserved upon himself and paid our penalty in his blood.

Read the following passages and prayerfully respond to the question below.

Love . . . rejoices with the truth. (1 Corinthians 13:6)

Speaking the truth in love, we will grow to become in every respect the mature body of [Christ], who is the head. (Ephesians 4:15)

QUESTION: According to these passages, what is the relationship between love and truth?

Reflect on these quotes from the *10 Words* book:

Truth and love are inseparable. However, today, in our "post-truth" world, love is scandalously separated from truth, not only in the fallen world but increasingly also in the church. We are told, for example, that by refusing to affirm people's sinful choices or chosen sexual "identities," we are not "loving," while speaking truthfully will brand you a "hater."

Today, many evangelicals equate love with being nice. But in practice, "niceness" means not speaking out against false and destructive cultural trends and beliefs, particularly those held by influential people. People who think this way say that they want nonbelievers to think well of them and presumably be more open to the gospel. But this is an illusion. Dividing truth from love will give you neither.

"Many Christian leaders have accepted this false notion that "winsomeness" and "being nice" are the best ways to win people over to the faith and not to speak clearly about moral truth. It is a great mistake because the loving thing to do is to tell the truth. If you love someone, you must tell the truth because you don't want them to persist in the lie that harms and damages them."—James Davidson Hunter[4]

"Biblical truth is the highest love for human beings."—Kelly Monroe Kullburg[5]

LEARNING TOGETHER: *LOVE*
Welcome and Opening Prayer

Opening Discussion
Discuss together what you learned about love during your personal study. What ideas stood out to you? How did God speak to you through the Scriptures?

Watch the Video and Discuss the Questions Below
Note: You'll find the "love" video at 10WordsBook.org.

- What insights did you gain from the video about love?
- What insights did you gain about the redefinition of love?

Definitions and Discussion
Read the two definitions and quotes below. Discuss the contemporary redefinition of love and its cultural consequences.

LOVE
(1) A source of pleasure, joy, or delight. (2) A strong affection, often accompanied by romantic feelings and sexual attraction. (3) To value, cherish, or treasure. (4) Fidelity and devotion. Faithful commitment. (5) To seek the good of another, to give for his or her benefit, even at a significant personal cost.

LOVE REDEFINED
(1) A source of pleasure, joy, or delight. (2) A strong affection, often accompanied by romantic feelings and sexual attraction.

Reflect on these quotes from the *10 Words* book:
What happens to love when a person, a society, or a culture abandons God? It becomes flat and one-dimensional. It loses its depth, richness, and power. Stripped of its essential qualities, it ceases to be genuine love and

becomes a destructive counterfeit. Tragically, this is what is happening in the post-Christian, post-truth West. Love has been reduced to little more than intense feelings of romantic affection and sexual attraction.

What's missing from this stripped-down, counterfeit version of "love"? Only the most profound aspects. Truth is gone. Fidelity, or covenant faithfulness, is also gone. And finally, gone is the most profound aspect of love, agape, or sacrificial service for the good of another. With agape stripped away, so are its corollaries: grace, mercy, compassion, and forgiveness. All that remains is an emotion-driven, self-centered narcissism and decadence that isn't love at all.

Because counterfeit love rejects God, it also rejects the God-ordained order of love, twisting love into a destructive idolatry. The love of money, pleasure, power, or fame replaces God at the top of the hierarchy. Disordered love is a narcissistic, emotion-driven, hedonistic counterfeit. It promises happiness, but that promise is a mirage. No amount of illicit sex, money, power, or fame can satisfy our deepest human needs. Idolizing these false gods leaves people empty, broken, and ultimately destroyed.

Discussion Questions
- How does the redefinition of love differ from the true definition? Discuss all that has changed.
- In what ways have you seen or experienced the redefinition of love?
- What are some of the social and cultural changes that the redefinition of love has brought about? What kinds of changes have resulted in policies and laws?

Personal Reflection and Application
Next week at home, take time to reflect on these areas of application. Read the questions and write down your responses.

Reflect on your understanding and practice of love.

Genuine love is not emotion driven. It is driven by our will, regardless of our feelings. We choose to love, even when we don't feel like it. We don't allow emotions to drive us because emotions are unsteady. They come and go. If our love were based entirely on feelings, it would be inconsistent and conditional, but that is not the nature of love. Genuine love is firm, consistent, faithful, and unconditional.

QUESTION: Reflect on your understanding and practice of love. Does it tend to be feelings-driven? Consider these questions: Have you ever ended a relationship because you no longer had the same feelings you once did? Have you ever failed to love your neighbor because you didn't feel like it? Have you ever failed to love someone hostile to you because of hatred or bitterness?

Because emotions are so powerful, choosing to love others without regard to feelings is so challenging; we can't do it in our strength alone. We need God to help and strengthen us. He will be more than happy to supply us with the power necessary to exercise genuine love.

QUESTION: Do you need God's help to love someone in your life as you should, regardless of your feelings? Confess your failure to love as you ought and ask God for the help and strength you need.

While love is not emotions-driven, some Christians overreact by claiming that love has nothing to do with feelings. This is false. Feelings such as affection, joy, and delight are central to love. To separate love from our emotions does irreparable damage to the concept. *The proper balance is understanding that feelings and emotions are central to love but cannot drive love. Our free choice is the engine that drives the train, and the feelings and emotions must follow, as they inevitably will.*

QUESTION: Does your own understanding of love discount feelings and emotions? Do you see love primarily as a duty and a matter of obedience? How can you kindle these feelings for others to love as you ought? Ask God for help in this area. You can even feel affection for an enemy when you realize that God loves them so much that he was willing to give his life that they might live.

Equating love with "being nice"

Equating love with niceness is perhaps the most widespread and destructive confusion about love in our churches. The basic idea is that Christians should be kind, gentle, and respectful, which is true. Still, the idea goes beyond this to affirm sinful and false beliefs and destructive behaviors.

When challenged, advocates of this so-called "winsome" approach to love will respond that Jesus loved and affirmed sinners. Yes, he did, but he didn't affirm their sin. Jesus told them that what they were doing was sinful and called them to repent (see John 8:1–11). He spoke truthfully about sin and, at the same time, loved sinful people.

Separating truth from love destroys love. As the apostle Paul says, we must "speak the truth in love" (Ephesians 4:15) and avoid the temptation to divide the two. The false understanding of love as "niceness" separates truth from love for fear of being seen as harsh or offensive, which, advocates claim, will harm our gospel witness.

However, this turns being nice into a utilitarian means to the end of evangelism. Evangelism is essential, *but it is not the highest end.* Love is. Love is the highest calling and duty of every Christian. What if the people we evangelize are not open to the gospel or refuse our invitation to attend church? Does that excuse us from loving them?

The evangelical church has taken something essential—evangelism—and made it something ultimate, and this is the source of many of its problems. Evangelism is a means to a larger end. It is about converting people into Christ-followers, who must be carefully discipled to love as he loved. That is the end.

QUESTION: Does your understanding of love move you to keep silent about sinful issues for fear of being seen as offensive or divisive? Have you used evangelism to justify this response? How might you change your thinking and practice to uphold truth and love together?

The proper ordering of love

If we are honest, many of us are like the rich man described in Matthew 19:16–22. He loved God but was unwilling to put him first in his heart, ahead of his wealth. When Jesus asked him to "sell [his] possessions and give to the poor," he was unwilling to make the sacrifice.

QUESTION: Do you have other "gods" (or idols) you are devoted to more than God? Do you love things, like wealth, more than you love God or people made in his image?

Sacrifice is required if we love something or someone more than God. This kind of sacrifice is nearly impossible when we focus on what we are giving up. It is much easier, however, when we focus on what we gain—namely, the eternal and abundant, joy-filled life God intended for us (John 10:10). What we gain is so valuable that, by comparison, we lose nothing and gain everything.

Here's how Jesus taught us to think about this trade-off:

> "The kingdom of heaven is like a treasure hidden in a field. When a man found it, he hid it again, and then in his joy went and sold all he had and bought that field. Again, the kingdom of heaven is like a merchant looking for fine pearls. When he found one of great value, he went away and sold everything he had and bought it" (Matthew 13:44–46).

Or, in the words of pastor John Piper, "Deny yourself the short, unsatisfying pleasures of the world so that you can have fullness of joy and pleasures forevermore at God's right hand."[6]

QUESTION: What do you need to "sell" or give up to rightly order God and his kingdom at the pinnacle of your love and devotion?

Loving your neighbor

Loving our neighbor is our highest moral duty after loving God. As the apostles made abundantly clear, the two are inextricably linked because all people bear God's image and have immeasurable worth (1 John 4:20). In the parable of the Good Samaritan, Jesus defined "neighbor" as anyone who is broken, hurting, and abandoned alongside the "road of life." Love for neighbors involves compassionate, sacrificial action on their behalf with no expectation of repayment.

QUESTION: Do you "see" the hurting, broken, and neglected people around you, or are you too busy with your daily life and agendas to notice them?

QUESTION: What practical actions can you take to "suffer together with the hurting, broken and neglected people in your life—perhaps even in your family? Are you prepared to get your hands dirty, minister to their needs, and heal their wounds, even if they are your enemies?

QUESTION: What groups or organizations exist in your community to serve the neglected, overlooked, needy, abused, and mistreated? How can you come alongside them to support their work?

Concluding Thoughts

"Christian faith involves trusting that at the center of the universe is a Being overflowing with love for His world. This means that the purpose of human existence is to receive this love, which has come to us in Jesus, and then give it back to others, creating an ecosystem of other-focused, self-giving love."—The Bible Project[7]

"To love another person is to see the face of God."[8]

RECOMMENDED RESOURCES

Books

- *The Four Loves* by C. S. Lewis (HarperOne, 2017)
- *No Greater Love: Experiencing the Heart of Jesus through the Gospel of John* by A.W. Tozer (Bethany House, 2020)
- *If Jesus Were Mayor: How Your Local Church Can Transform Your Community* by Bob Moffitt (Monarch Books, 2004)
- *When Helping Hurts: How to Alleviate Poverty Without Hurting the Poor . . . and Yourself* by Steve Corbett and Brian Fikkert (Moody Publishing, 2004)

Curriculum

I recommend two outstanding practical resources developed by Bob Moffitt, president of the Harvest Foundation, to help churches and individuals put love into practice: *Seed Projects* and *Disciplines of Love.* These free resources are available on the Harvest website: harvestfoundation.org/curriculum/materials/.

Videos

- The Bible Project: Ahavah-Love
  bibleproject.com/explore/video/ahavah-love/
- The Bible Project: Agape-Love
  bibleproject.com/explore/video/agape-love/

Scott David Allen is president of the Disciple Nations Alliance. He is a frequent teacher on topics ranging from Christianity and culture to worldview, family, biblical justice, and poverty. He has authored and coauthored numerous books, including his bestselling book *Why Social Justice Is Not Biblical Justice: An Urgent Appeal to Fellow Christians in a Time of Social Crisis.*

Before serving as president of the Disciple Nations Alliance, Scott served for 19 years with the Christian poverty alleviation organization Food for the Hungry.

He has traveled extensively in Africa, Asia, and Latin America, equipping Christian leaders to embrace a biblical worldview and to live it out personally and publicly in faithfulness to Christ's command to make disciples of all nations.

He and his wife, Kimberly, live in Bend, Oregon. Scott is the proud father of five children and has three grandchildren.

CHAPTER 1: TRUTH

1. John 18:38.
2. [2] Charles J. Chaput, "The Splendor of Truth in 2017," First Things, October 2017, firstthings.com/article/2017/10/the-splendor-of-truth-in-2017.
3. Sinan Aral, "How Lies Spread Online," The New York Times, March 8, 2018, nytimes.com/2018/03/08/opinion/sunday/truth-lies-spread-online.html.
4. The actual quote is, "Against [empiricism], which halts at [observable] phenomena—'There are only facts'—I would say, no, facts is precisely what there is not, only interpretations. We cannot establish any fact 'in itself': perhaps it is folly to want to do such a thing." In "Nietzsche on the Impossibility of Truth," neamathisi.com/new-learning/chapter-7-knowledge-and-learning/nietzsche-on-the-impossibility-of-truth.
5. Allan Bloom, The Closing of the American Mind: How Higher Education Has Failed Democracy and Impoverished the Souls of Today's Students (New York: Simon and Schuster, 1987), 25.
6. Amy B. Wang, "'Post-truth' named 2016 word of the year by Oxford Dictionaries," Washington Post, November 16, 2016, washingtonpost.com/news/the-fix/wp/2016/11/16/post-truth-named-2016-word-of-the-year-by-oxford-dictionaries/?utm_term=.c3eee5f38a90.
7. Nancy Pearcey, Finding Truth: 5 Principles for Unmasking Atheism, Secularism, and Other God Substitutes (Colorado Springs: David C. Cook, 2015), 120.
8. Quoted in "1984 Philosophical Viewpoints Quotes," shmoop.com/1984/philosophical-viewpoints-quotes-3.html.
9. The English word repent comes from the Greek word metanoia, which literally means "change your mind." Change the way you think. Change your assumptions and allow your actions and behaviors to follow. This is how we use the word repent in this course.
10. Michael Novak, "Truth and Freedom," First Things, January 2, 2009, firstthings.com/web-exclusives/2009/01/truth-and-freedom.
11. Archbishop Charles Chaput, "The priests we need," October 6, 2016, CatholicPhilly.com, catholicphilly.com/2016/10/homilies-speeches/the-priests-we-need/.
12. J. I. Packer, Fundamentalism and the Word of God (Grand Rapids: Eerdmans Publishing Co., 1958), 34.

CHAPTER 2: HUMAN

1. Malcolm Muggeridge, *Something Beautiful for God* (New York: Ballantine Books edition, 1971), 15.
2. A popular translation. Here is another: "You stir us so that praising you may bring us joy, because you have made us and draw us to yourself, and our heart is unquiet until it rests in you," Maria Boulding, translator, Augustine, Confessions, 1.1 (New York: New City Press, 1997), 14.
3. James K. A. Smith, *Letters to a Young Calvinist: An Invitation to the Reformed Tradition* (Grand Rapids: Brazos Press, 2010), 109.
4. Justin Taylor, "Aleksandr Solzhenitsyn: 'Bless You, Prison!'" The Gospel Coalition, October 14, 2011, thegospelcoalition.org/blogs/justin-taylor/aleksandr-solzhenitsyn-bless-you-prison/.
5. linkedin.com/pulse/growing-deep-christian-life-12-exposing-dark-side-wayne-raley/.
6. William B. Provine, "Darwinism: Science or Naturalistic Philosophy?" in a debate with Phillip E. Johnson, April 30, 1994, quoted in "God Questions—a dialogue," Carl Stecher and Peter S. Williams, bethinking.org, bethinking.org/does-god-exist/god-questions-a-dialogue/4-problem-of-evil.
7. Wesley J. Smith, *A Rat Is a Pig Is a Dog Is a Boy: The Human Cost of the Animal Rights Movement* (New York: Encounter Books, 2010).
8. Carl R. Trueman, "A Medieval Perspective on Modern Identity Politics," *First Things*, January 2, 2015, firstthings.com/blogs/firstthoughts/2015/01/modern-identity-politics-a-medieval-perspective.
9. Jeremy Rifkin, Algen, *A New Word—A New World* (New York: Viking, 1983), 244, quoted in D. A. Carson, *Christ and Culture Revisited* (Grand Rapids: Wm. B. Eerdmans Publishing Co., 2008), 89.
10. Nancy Pearcey, *Finding Truth* (Colorado Springs: David C. Cook, 2015), 118.
11. Rodney Stark, "The Rise of Christianity: A Sociologist Reconsiders History," *Frontline*, pbs.org/wgbh/pages/frontline/shows/religion/why/starktheology.html.
12. thegospelcoalition.org/blogs/justin-taylor/there-are-no-ordinary-people-you-have-never-talked-to-a-mere-mortal/.

CHAPTER 3: SEX

1. Nancy Pearcey, *Love Thy Body: Answering Hard Questions about Life and Sexuality* (Grand Rapids: Baker Books, 2018), 29.
2. Timothy Keller with Kathy Keller, *The Meaning of Marriage: Facing the Complexities of Commitment with the Wisdom of God* (New York: Penguin Books, 2013), 257.
3. Rod Dreher, "Sex After Christianity: Gay marriage is not just a social revolution but a cosmological one," *The American Conservative*, April 11, 2013, theamericanconservative.com/articles/sex-after-christianity/.

4. Todd Wilson, *Mere Sexuality: Rediscovering the Christian Vision of Sexuality* (Grand Rapids: Zondervan, 2017), 30.

5. Wilson, 100–101.

6. Alex Morris, "Tales from the Millennials' Sexual Revolution," *Rolling Stone*, March 31, 2014, rollingstone.com/feature/millennial-sexual-revolution-relationships-marriage.

7. Margaret Sanger, Michael W. Perry, H. G. Wells (2003), *The Pivot of Civilization in Historical Perspective: The Birth Control Classic*, Inkling Books, 406.

8. Wilson, 38.

CHAPTER 4: MARRIAGE

1. Doug Mainwaring (March 7, 2017). Your Marriage. You Have No Idea of the Good You Are Doing. *Public Discourse*. thepublicdiscourse.com/2017/03/18600/.

2. J. R. Miller, *Home-Making* (San Antonio: The Vision Forum, Inc., 2001, originally published 1882), 34, 38.

3. John Piper, *This Momentary Marriage: A Parable of Permanence* (Wheaton, IL: Crossway Books), 2009, 101.

4. This definition is based on one provided by Ryan Anderson in "Why Marriage Matters Most," The Heritage Foundation, July 10, 2013, heritage.org/marriage-and-family/commentary/why-marriage-matters-most.

5. "Premarital Sex Is Nearly Universal Among Americans, and Has Been for Decades," Guttmacher Institute, December 19, 2006, guttmacher.org/news-release/2006/premarital-sex-nearly-universal-among-americans-and-has-been-decades.

6. Katherine Kersten, "The risks of cohabitation," Center of the American Experiment, April 4, 2011, americanexperiment.org/article/the-risks-of-cohabitation/.

7. Bella DePaulo, "What Is the Divorce Rate, Really?" *Psychology Today*, February 2, 2017, psychologytoday.com/us/blog/living-single/201702/what-is-the-divorce-rate-really.

8. Todd Wilson, *Mere Sexuality: Rediscovering the Christian Vision of Sexuality* (Grand Rapids: Zondervan, 2017), 79.

9. Sean McDowell and John Stonestreet, *Same-Sex Marriage: A Thoughtful Approach to God's Design for Marriage* (Grand Rapids: Baker Books, 2014), 100.

CHAPTER 5: FREEDOM

1. Stiles J. Watson, Chalcedon Foundation, "Biblical Self-Government," September 18, 2007, chalcedon.edu/resources/articles/biblical-self-government.

2. Brad Littlejohn, "Ahmari among the Protestants," *American Reformer*, americanreformer.org/2022/02/ahmari-among-the-protestants/.

3. Taken from this webpage: edmundburkeinstitute.ie/who-was-edmund-burke/.

4. Hunter Baker, "Habermas on Christianity, Europe, and Human Rights," June 3, 2009, Acton Institute, blog.acton.org/archives/10604-habermas-on-christianity-europe-and-human-rights.html.
5. lexico.com/en/definition/freedom.
6. Quoted in Cornell Law School, Legal Information Institute, law.cornell.edu/supct/html/91–744.ZO.html.
7. John Zmirak, "Planned Parenthood and the Gift of Death," *The Stream*, August 26, 2015, stream.org/planned-parenthood-gift-death/.
8. Paul Kingsnorth, "The Cross and the Machine," *First Things*, June 2021, firstthings.com/article/2021/06/the-cross-and-the-machine.
9. blog.acton.org/archives/100574-the-logic-of-the-soul-6-quotes-from-whittaker-chambers-letter-to-my-children.html.
10. Ronald Reagan, Freedom Speech, reagan.com/ronald-reagan-freedom-speech.

CHAPTER 7: JUSTICE

1. Martin Luther King Jr. Letter from Birmingham Jail. billofrightsinstitute.org/primary-sources/letter-from-birmingham-jail.
2. Tim Keller, "What Is Biblical Justice?" *Relevant*, August 23, 2012.
3. Justin Taylor, "Aleksandr Solzhenitsyn: 'Bless You, Prison!'" The Gospel Coalition, October 14, 2011, thegospelcoalition.org/blogs/justin-taylor/aleksandr-solzhenitsyn-bless-you-prison/.
4. Quoted in Al Mohler, "Why Religion, If Not Based in Truth, Is Grounded in Nothing More Than Moral Aspirations," The Briefing, December 19, 2018, albertmohler.com/2018/12/19/briefing-12-19-18/.
5. From the back cover of *Why Social Justice is Not Biblical Justice: An Urgent Appeal to Fellow Christians in a Time of Social Crisis* by Scott D. Allen (Grand Rapids: Credo House Publishing), 2020.

CHAPTER 8: FAITH

1. merriam-webster.com/dictionary/faith.
2. gotquestions.org/trust-the-Bible.html.
3. If you'd like to learn more about the amazing advances in science that point to the necessity for a Creator-God, there are many excellent resources, but I recommend starting with *Is Atheism Dead?* By Eric Metaxas (Salem Books, October 2021).
4. There is overwhelming evidence in the historical reliability and truthfulness of the Bible. If you'd like to learn more about it, there are many outstanding resources. I recommend starting with *The Case for Christ: A Journalist's Personal Investigation of the Evidence for Jesus* by Lee Strobel (Zondervan, 2016). *Evidence That Demands a Verdict: Life-Changing Truth for a Skeptical World* by Josh McDowell and Sean McDowell (Thomas Nelson, 2017), and *Unearthing the Bible: 101 Archaeological Discoveries That Bring the Bible to Life* by Titus Kennedy (Harvest House Publishers, 2020).

5. 10 Key Bible Verses on Faith," Crossway, March 26, 2020, crossway.org/articles/10-key-bible-verses-on-faith/.

6. Russell, Bertrand. "Will Religious Faith Cure Our Troubles?" Human Society in Ethics and Politics. Archived from the original on 2020-11-12. Retrieved 16 August 2009.

7. crossway.org/articles/10-key-bible-verses-on-faith/.

CHAPTER 9: BEAUTY

1. Jerry Root and Stan Guthrie, *The Sacrament of Evangelism* (Chicago: Moody Publishers, 2011), 194–195.

2. Elizabeth Lev, *How Catholic Art Saved the Faith: The Triumph of Beauty and Truth in Counter Reformation Art*, 2019.

3. J. R. R. Tolkien, On Fairy-Stories, eds. Verlyn Flieger and Douglas A. Anderson (London: HarperCollins, 2014), 47–55.

4. C. S. Lewis, quoted by Chuck Colson and Nancy Pearcey in *How Now Shall We Live?* (Wheaton, IL: Tyndale House Publishers, Inc., 1999), 449.

5. Robert Florzak, "Why Is Modern Art So Bad?" prageru.com/video/why-is-modern-art-so-bad.

6. goodreads.com/quotes/1194450-beauty-is-no-quality-in-things-themselves-it-exists-merely.

7. David Taylor, "A Holy Longing: Beauty is the hard-to-define essence that draws people to the gospel," *Christianity Today*, October 2008, christianitytoday.com/ct/2008/october/17.39.html.

CHAPTER 10: LOVE

1. Alyssa Roat, "What Is Agape Love? Bible Meaning and Examples," Christianity.com, April 17, 2024, christianity.com/wiki/christian-terms/what-does-agape-love-really-mean-in-the-bible.html.

2. For the original passage and wording, see Nick Nowalk, "Pascal's God-Shaped Hole," ichthus, May 2, 2011, harvardichthus.org/2011/05/pascal_hole/.

3. Noah Webster, "Love," 1828 Dictionary, webstersdictionary1828.com/Dictionary/love.

4. "Author John Daniel Davidson says that paganism in America is on the rise," The Tucker Carlson Podcast, April 30, 2024, tuckercarlson.com/listen/.

5. christianitytoday.com/2015/04/unexpected-defenders-meet-women-apologists/.

6. John Piper, "Joy Changes Everything: An Invitation to Christian Hedonism," Champion Forest Baptist Church, Houston, November 12, 2017, desiringgod.org/messages/joy-changes-everything.

7. "Agape-Love," BibleProject, December 21, 2017, bibleproject.com/explore/video/agape-love/.

8. A quote from Victor Hugo's novel *Les Misérables*.

CONTINUE YOUR JOURNEY

Q 10wordsbook.org

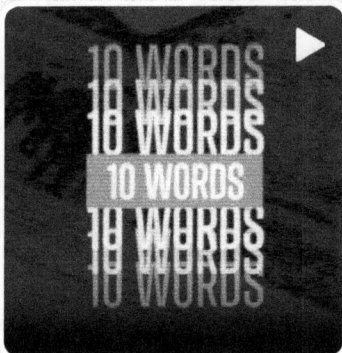

BIBLE STUDY

This study guide is designed for small group Bible study and is built around a ten-part short video series and thoughtful discussion questions.

PODCAST

Join Scott on the *Ideas Have Consequences* podcast as he discusses each of the ten words from the book. The podcast is a great way to introduce people to the book and study guide.

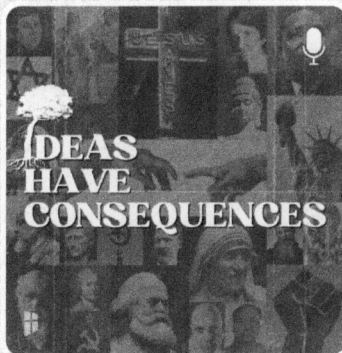

ABOUT THE DISCIPLE NATIONS ALLIANCE

disciplenations.org

Nations, communities, families, and people are broken and crying out for hope, healing, and restoration. God blessed His people, the Church, to be His ambassadors in reconciling and restoring the broken nations of this world.

Our vision at the Disciple Nations Alliance is to see blessed nations profoundly shaped by biblical truth in ways that lead to freedom, justice, and human flourishing.

Learn how you can join the movement at *disciplenations.org*.

Disciple Nations Alliance

www.ingramcontent.com/pod-product-compliance
Lightning Source LLC
LaVergne TN
LVHW051401080426
835508LV00022B/2925